Texas State Lib

3 6237

MW00827790

Reference and Access

	DATE DUE	

Innovative Practices for Archives and Special Collections
Series Editor: Kate Theimer

This dynamic series is aimed at those working in archives and special collections as well as other cultural heritage organizations. It also provides students and faculty in archives, library, and public history graduate programs a resource for understanding the issues driving change in the field today.

Each book in the series tackles a different area in the field of archives and special collections librarianship and demonstrates the kinds of strategies archivists are using to meet these new challenges.

These innovative practices reflect approaches and ideas that will be new to many readers. The case studies featured in each book have been selected to keep in mind a broad spectrum of readers and enable the series, as a whole, to benefit a diverse audience.

Each book features case studies from both large and small organizations. Thus, some of the creative ideas presented are being implemented with costly tools and robust infrastructures, and others are being done on a shoestring. A hallmark of the series is that every case study incorporates ideas that are transferrable, even if the specific implementation might not be.

About the Series Editor

Kate Theimer is the author of the popular blog *ArchivesNext* and a frequent writer, speaker, and commentator on issues related to the future of archives. She is the author of *Web 2.0 Tools and Strategies for Archives and Local History Collections* and the editor of *A Different Kind of Web: New Connections between Archives and Our Users*, as well as having contributed chapters to *Many Happy Returns: Advocacy for Archives and Archivists*, *The Future of Archives and Recordkeeping* and the forthcoming *Encyclopedia of Archival Concepts, Principles, and Practices*. She has published articles in *The American Archivist* and the *Journal of Digital Humanities*.

Kate served on the Council of the Society of American Archivists from 2010 to 2013. Before starting her career as an independent writer and editor, she worked in the policy division of the National Archives and Records Administration in College Park, Maryland.

Reference and Access

Innovative Practices for Archives and Special Collections

Kate Theimer

ROWMAN & LITTLEFIELD
Lanham • Boulder • New York • Toronto • Plymouth, UK

Texas State Library
and Archives Commission
LIBRARY SCIENCE COLLECTION
Austin, Texas 78711

Published by Rowman & Littlefield
4501 Forbes Boulevard, Suite 200, Lanham, Maryland 20706
www.rowman.com

10 Thornbury Road, Plymouth PL6 7PP, United Kingdom

Copyright © 2014 by Rowman & Littlefield

All rights reserved. No part of this book may be reproduced in any form or by any
electronic or mechanical means, including information storage and retrieval systems,
without written permission from the publisher, except by a reviewer who may quote
passages in a review.

British Library Cataloguing in Publication Information Available

Library of Congress Cataloging-in-Publication Data

Reference and access / edited by Kate Theimer.
    pages cm. -- (Innovative practices for archives and special collections ; 3)
    Includes bibliographical references and index.
    ISBN 978-0-8108-9091-6 (pbk. : alk. paper) -- ISBN 978-0-8108-9092-3 (ebook) 1. Archives--
Reference services. 2. Libraries--Special collections. 3. Reference services (Libraries) 4. Information
storage and retrieval systems--Archival materials. 5. Archives--Reference services--Case studies. 6.
Libraries--Special collections--Case studies. 7. Reference services (Libraries)--Case studies. I.
Theimer, Kate, 1966- editor of compilation.
    CD971.R367 2014
    027--dc23
    2013049328

RECEIVED

JUN 1 7 2014

PURCHASING

∞™ The paper used in this publication meets the minimum requirements of American
National Standard for Information Sciences Permanence of Paper for Printed Library
Materials, ANSI/NISO Z39.48-1992.

Printed in the United States of America

Contents

Introduction

For most archivists and special collections librarians, serving the public by providing reference services and access to materials is the goal for which all other processes exist. The way archives address these needs has been affected by two related factors: changes in technology and an increased emphasis on meeting researcher needs. Many of the case studies in this volume reflect how those factors have inspired innovation, while others demonstrate the need to react to the realities of the current environment. Innovation in this area is thus fueled, as it often is, both by opportunities and evolutions in the organizational landscape.

Reference and Access: Innovative Practices for Archives and Special Collections explores how archives of different sizes and types are increasing their effectiveness in serving the public and meeting internal needs. The case studies in this collection demonstrate new ways to interact with users to answer their questions, provide access to materials, support patrons in the reading room, and manage reference and access processes. This volume is useful to those working in archives and special collections as well as other cultural heritage organizations and provides ideas ranging from the aspirational to the immediately implementable. It also provides students and educators in archives, library, and public history graduate programs a resource for understanding the issues driving change in the field today and the kinds of strategies archivists are using to meet these new challenges.

ABOUT THE INNOVATIVE PRACTICES SERIES

I debated with myself for some time over the title of this series, *Innovative Practices for Archives and Special Collections*. After all, what is innovative and new to one person is often standard procedure to another. Another option was to call them *best practices* and follow the model of a series of similar books from the same publisher featuring case studies from libraries, but this seemed equally problematic. In a field that seems to embrace the phrase "it depends" as a mantra, putting forward the experience of any one archive as best practice seemed ill advised.

It is the very diversity of our field, though, that caused me to stick with my *innovative* label rather than shying away from it. There are new ideas in these books or at least ideas that will be new to many readers.

My philosophy in selecting case studies for the books in this series has been to keep in mind a broad spectrum of readers and to position the series so that it is as valuable as possible for a diverse audience. In each book you will find case studies from both big organizations and small ones. Some of the creative ideas presented are being implemented with costly tools and robust infrastructures, and others are being done on a shoestring. In determining what to include, I wanted to ensure that every case study incorporates ideas that are transferrable, even if the specific implementation might not be.

This commitment to making the series broadly valuable and practical has meant striving for a balance that favors more approachable innovations over implementations that are aggressively on the "cutting edge." The ideas presented here are within the reach of most archives and special collections, if not right away, then in the near future. They represent the creativity and commitment to serving and expanding our audiences that I think are the defining characteristics of the archival profession in the early twenty-first century.

Because archival functions and processes are interrelated and don't always fit neatly into compartments and because most archivists perform several of them in the course of their daily work, the contents of each of the volumes in this series has both its own clear focus and overlapping relationships with the others. Case studies in reference and access touch inevitably on description and outreach. Because the overarching purpose of description is to facilitate use, issues relating to reference, access, and outreach are components of the case studies in that volume. The overlap of the management volume with all of the others should not be surprising, though the focus of the case studies there are more explicitly on management issues. These interrelationships are inevitable given the nature of archival work, and most practitioners and students will find all of the volumes useful.

Just as the activities archivists undertake depend on each other, so have I depended on the assistance of my friends and colleagues, who generously agreed to review the case studies. My thanks to Rodney Carter, Amy Cooper Cary, Jim Gerencser, Mary Manning, and Tanya Zanish-Belcher for the time and careful consideration they have given to improving the books in this series.

ABOUT THE REFERENCE AND ACCESS CASE STUDIES

Deconstructing reference and access services into their essential elements and including case studies that addressed all of these elements provided an overarching rationale for the selection of contributions to this volume. In a broad sense, providing reference and access services for users consists of:

- interacting with people who have questions,
- providing access to materials that meet researcher needs,
- assisting researchers as they use materials, and
- managing the processes needed to support reference and access.

Although certainly it's possible to consider other activities as part of an active reference program, as Mary Jo Pugh does in *Providing Reference Services for Archives & Manuscripts*, these four areas seem to me to encapsulate the essential aspects of the function. In what ways, then, has archivists' support for these activities changed, and how do the case studies in this collection demonstrate innovation in these areas?

First, how has the way people approach archives to ask questions changed? In many ways, this area of reference remains largely the same. Researchers still ask questions in person in the reading room and via e-mail, telephone, and "snail mail" inquiries, however they now also pose questions on social media sites, such as blogs, Twitter, and Facebook. Interacting with the public on social media often has a reference as well as an outreach component. In this collection, Gary Brannan's case study about the West Yorkshire Archive Service and its use of scheduled open webchats to answer researcher questions represents a new way of serving remote audiences and interacting in real time. In their wide-ranging case study on reviewing and updating reference systems, Jackie Couture and Deborah Whalen include implementing a webchat widget on their archives website, a practice often found today on academic library sites.

These examples illustrate different ways of interacting to answer the questions of off-site patrons. But how have interactions during a reference interview taking place in the reading room changed? Again, in many ways this kind of exchange remains fundamentally the same, but technologies can improve how archivists help researchers discover new collections. In their case study about the introduction of iPads into the reading room, Cheryl Oestreicher, Julia Stringfellow, and Jim Duran discuss how being able to use a portable tablet to start users off on their exploration of online resources supports easier discovery of relevant resources in the physical collection.

The area that has undoubtedly seen the most change has been how archivists provide access to materials researchers need. Technology has been the primary catalyst and, when combined with a drive to actively make materials available before users ask for them, has resulted in many innovative practices designed to allow users to meet their own needs without mediation by archivists. Sara Snyder and Elizabeth Botten's case study about integrating reference into usability testing for the Archives of American Art website illustrates the importance of treating a website as an interface for reference and one in which people can ideally fulfill many of their own information needs without the participation of an archivist. Jennie Levine Knies's articulation of the University of Maryland's exploration of enhancing access to collections through collaboration in digital humanities projects demonstrates the potential for increased discovery and analysis of archival materials when they are made available in diverse "publishing" models. And Lisa Snider eloquently reminds us that access to materials via our websites, of course, needs to be designed to accommodate the full range of differently abled users.

Archivists have also used technology to establish new ways of making materials available in response to researcher interest. In her case study, Michelle Light discusses her approach to a new set of challenges in creating a web equivalent for a physical reading room in which to make two collections of born-digital materials available. In other cases, access can be made possible by something as simple as the acquisition of new scanning equipment together with expanded digitization policies, as Melanie Griffin and Matthew Knight's case study describes. The avenues that digitization, both on demand and as part of a program, present for increased access are clear and well known, but as digitization programs in archives mature, it is interesting to see them become more integrated with other archival services, including reference. Greater input from both reference and processing staff into digitization priorities is one of many ways Emily Christopherson and Rachael Dreyer describe for strategically meeting researcher needs in a repository dedicated to the "More Product, Less Process" (MPLP) philosophy.

Another traditional part of providing access has been the work the archivist does to assist researchers in identifying relevant materials, either before or after the researcher is on site. The impact of MPLP on processing programs has been actively discussed in the literature, but assessments of the changes it necessitates in reference services are less common. Again the Christopherson and Dreyer case study dissects the ways in which three departments at the American Heritage Center (AHC)—reference, processing, and digitization—must all work together to provide the best possible experience for researchers working with varying levels of collection description. The heaviest burden for working with researchers falls on reference staff, as one would expect, and the archivists at AHC have explored a variety of creative strategies for providing the best possible reference experience for users. Marc Brodsky addresses a different aspect of the problem of mediating reference questions, asking how processes for training new reference archivists can be improved so that new staff can more quickly and efficiently become proficient in assisting researchers to locate relevant materials in their repository's unique collections.

While technology and increased scanning mean that many researchers no longer need to visit a repository in person, for many patrons archival research still means spending time in the reading room. Here again, while much remains the same, archivists are adopting and adapting technology to help improve that experience. While making iPads freely available to users (as described by Boise State University archivists) and allowing unlimited access to an advanced scanner in the reading room (at the University of South Florida) seem like simple changes, the immediate benefits for both patrons and staff may be surprising.

But there are some problems that technology can't solve on its own. While few archives or special collections will face exactly the same challenge Leanda Gahegan and Gina Rappaport did when the Smithsonian's National Anthropological Archives hosted the Breath of Life Archival Institute for Indigenous Languages, many may have occasion to host large groups of researchers—often larger than the available space can accommodate—for short periods of intense work. These authors also had to address the need to interact appropriately and respectfully with Native American researchers examining their own communities' legacies as embodied in archival collections. These combined challenges required Gahegan and Rappaport to modify some standard reading room policies and also to familiarize themselves with some new best practices, including the *Protocols for Native American Archival Materials*.

In addition to helping patrons in the reading room, archivists must also monitor their activities and enforce policies that create a secure environment for the use of valuable materials. Sometimes it takes an unfortunate loss to make an organization review and update security policies. In their case study, Elizabeth Chase, Gabrielle M. Dudley, and Sara Logue describe how the Manuscript, Archives, and Rare Book Library at Emory University identified and enforced a new suite of security procedures as well as how those new procedures were viewed by researchers and staff.

All of the processes through which archivists provide reference assistance and access to materials need, of course, to be managed. Proper policies, procedures, workflows, and infrastructure are as necessary for a successful reference program as a knowledgeable and user-focused staff. While revising and implementing new policies and systems may seem like an intimidating prospect, Jackie Couture and Deborah Whalen explain how they successfully tackled it at Eastern Kentucky University using only the resources they had available or could obtain for free. Many of the other cases studies in this volume also include elements that might be properly considered in the realm of "management": Light discusses copyright and donor relations, Christopherson and Dreyer address interdepartmental cooperation and communicating with donors, Knies explores establishing successful collaborative relationships with faculty and technology colleagues, and Brodksy discusses training of new staff. Other case studies describe how existing policies are evaluated and how new policies are created and implemented. In addition, Snider's recommendations for increasing usability of archives' websites and Snyder and Botten's introduction to conducting website usability testing clearly are of value to managers responsible for services including and beyond reference and access.

While each case study in this collection describes a specific response to a challenge or opportunity, I think each also reflects a philosophy of experimentation that is perhaps the most critical ingredient necessary for any organization interested in developing its own "innovative" practices. In this regard I hope this book and the others in the series encourage all readers to consider how their own work could benefit from the exploration of new ideas and tools. The books in this series can, by definition, include only a small sample of the kinds of approaches being developed by archives and special collections around the world to meet the challenges of staying relevant and adaptable in today's complex environment. These case studies will give readers many useful ideas to consider as well as the inspiration to come up with tomorrow's innovations.

ONE
Building Bridges

*Closing the Divide between Minimally Processed
Collections and Researchers*

Emily Christopherson and Rachael Dreyer,
American Heritage Center

Minimal processing contributes many new cubic feet of collection material to the body of content available for researchers, allowing scholars to
explore new theories for which they might otherwise not be able to locate
evidence hidden within undescribed collections and materials. However,
minimal processing also creates a rather unique set of challenges for
archivists who work directly with those researchers. The "More Product,
Less Process" (MPLP)[1] approach frequently presents challenges for reference archivists in the form of the competing interests of MPLP processing
and researchers' use of collections. Tensions arise between the level of
detail that researchers require and the degree of detail to which the processing archivists have inventoried collections. Because the University of
Wyoming's American Heritage Center (AHC) was an early adopter of the
MPLP methodology, our reference staff has experienced a range of issues
caused by the disconnect between user needs and implementing more
efficient processing workflows. Our experience has led us to develop a
variety of strategies to address these tensions based on greater collaboration across functional areas. Collaboration between the reference and
processing departments is naturally a primary focus, but we have also
seen benefits from changing workflows in our accessioning and digital
programs departments as well.

Interdepartmental cooperation not only has allowed the AHC to provide greater access to its collections but also to direct our efforts toward collections that receive the most use. In an era of limited resources and a desire for wider access, it can be a struggle to meet both internal demands of efficiency and external expectations for increasing levels of service. However, increasing the dialogue between the AHC's two largest departments (reference and processing) has allowed us to address this challenge and ease the impacts of MPLP processing on our reference services. This case study discusses the kinds of problems our reference department experienced and how we worked with colleagues in other departments across the organization to come up with creative solutions to ensure users' needs are being met. What has emerged is an organization in which there is greater cross-training for members of all departments, giving us more flexible job responsibilities, all while focusing on the needs of our end users.

PLANNING

Many of the changes in workflow made in all departments at the AHC over the past ten years in response to the implementation of MPLP have been made gradually and in response to situations and concerns as they arose. In consequence, their implementation occasionally produced results with unintended consequences for colleagues in other departments. This section first provides a brief overview of MPLP as implemented at the AHC. It then briefly describes the processing and reference departments at the AHC, including the issues that arose from the implementation of MPLP that predicated a change in workflow for members of both departments.

The MPLP approach outlined by Greene and Meissner in their seminal article provides a very flexible framework for processing. There are many ways it can be implemented at a particular institution to best fit that repository's problems, priorities, and goals. The main objective of MPLP is to focus resources on getting as many collections visible and usable to researchers as quickly as possible. Part of this focus is to decrease or eliminate processing backlogs by establishing minimal levels of processing and to establish policies that drive spending more time and effort on materials that require it based on user needs. It is important to understand that MPLP does not advocate that all collections be processed at the same minimal level. It emphasizes the need for flexibility in processing and making decisions on a collection-to-collection basis as to the appropriate level of processing.[2] These decisions should be based on a variety of factors, including available resources, use, and importance of each particular collection. This flexibility allows MPLP guidelines to be implemented in the way that best fits each individual repository. Furthermore, if a collection is processed at a minimal level that later turns out to have been inadequate, it is acceptable to then reprocess the collection at a more detailed level. While it is true that MPLP generally advocates description at a less discrete level, it also acknowledges that there are collections and circumstances that warrant a more detailed level of processing. MPLP simply states that a number of factors, including use, importance, and size of a collection, should be considered and that your resources should then be allocated accordingly. Flexibility is a hallmark of the MPLP philosophy, and we took that to heart as we later tackled the challenges its implementation presented to those of us on the reference front lines.

Before discussing the more recent changes the AHC has made to increase interdepartmental collaboration, it may be helpful to first discuss the history of MPLP at the AHC. Since the publication of the original Greene and Meissner article, the AHC has made significant changes in how it processes collections. Indeed, as Mark Greene has been the director of the AHC since 2002, there is a good chance that we have practiced, experimented, and revised our processing workflows with regards to MPLP more so than most other repositories. This includes the completion of collection-level catalog records for all holdings, changes in accessioning procedure, and collaboration between the reference and processing departments in determining which collections to process. Prior to the implementation of MPLP, the AHC had 1,932 unprocessed collections, which were effectively hidden from researchers. Believing that making all collections known and findable by researchers was more important than ensuring that all collections opened to the public had sufficient finding aids, the AHC attacked its large backlog of uncataloged collections. In 2005–2006, with help from two National Historical Publications and Records Commission (NHPRC) grants, the AHC evaluated all unprocessed collections, marking each for retention and cataloging, administrative action, or deaccession review. After the evaluation, 28 percent of the collections received collection-level catalog records. This was approximately 537 collections, totaling 7,074 cubic feet. The remainder of the unprocessed collections were either merged with existing AHC collections or marked for deaccession.

Before going further, we would like to discuss what needs to be done to a collection in order for it to be considered "processed." *Processing* is a relative term, and archivists have developed varied definitions for fully processed, minimally processed, and unprocessed collections. How processed is a collection with only a catalog record? Is a finding aid required to consider a collection processed? Does the finding aid need to be DACS compliant and include a biography, scope and content note, and container listing? Is it processed when it can be used productively for research? Clearly, the meaning of *processed* varies. In fact, the terms *processed* and *unprocessed* currently have little meaning at the AHC. Rather, the reality is that all collections are accessible to researchers, albeit with varying levels of description (of which we describe in more detail later), and all collections can later be reprocessed to a higher level of detail if a situation warrants it. However, for the purposes of this article, at the AHC any collection that has at least a catalog record is considered processed (very minimally so). As a result of the work made possible by the NHPRC grant, the AHC created catalog records for every permanent manuscript collection. At this point, while all collections were considered processed, some only had collection-level catalog records available as a guide for both researchers and reference staff. This posed one of the most difficult challenges to the reference staff in providing consistent and high-level service to patrons.

After that project was complete, the AHC revised its accessioning protocols to avoid building up another backlog of uncataloged collections. In the revised accessioning workflow, when a collection is first brought to the AHC, the accessioner creates a catalog record and brief EAD finding aid. This includes any biographical information easily found, a brief scope and content note, a short list of access terms, and a box-level container list. The container lists are very rudimentary and generally are not intellectually organized into series. At this stage the information provided is more focused on types of materials (scrapbooks, photographs, subject files, journals, and DVDs, for example) rather than the content or subject of the materials. This is due, in part, to the fact that this work is often done by the archival accessioner and student workers, not by members of the processing department.

While the catalog record and box listing are very rudimentary at this stage, as soon as the collections are shelved, they can immediately be found in a catalog search and accessed by researchers. During accessioning any access restrictions specified by the donor are clearly marked, and the boxes that contain these materials are identified. A notification is also entered into the AHC's electronic collection management system so that both processing and reference archivists will immediately be cognizant of the existence of restricted materials when issuing retrieval slips for requested collections. Other materials not specified by the donor that contain sensitive information may or may not be identified at this point, depending on if they are clearly labeled and/or noticed by the accessioner or her student aids. It is up to the reference and processing archivists to later identify these materials. For many collections (especially smaller ones), what takes place during accessioning may be the only processing they receive. Other collections may later be routed to the processing department to be reprocessed and given a more complete finding aid and content list.

Because collections are so quickly made available to researchers, often with only these very minimal–level finding aids, interdepartmental collaboration becomes essential between the reference department and the processing department to ensure satisfactory use of collection materials by our patrons.

A brief overview of our processes in the AHC's reference department is also important to understand why and how various changes were made to help us provide better service to our patrons for minimally processed collections. Each year, the AHC assists a diverse range of on-site and distance researchers. The reference department offers repository tours as well as research orientation sessions for University of Wyoming undergraduate classes and for Laramie County Community College courses. Tours and research assistance are also available for K–12 audiences as well; while some of these tours and orientations are tailored for National History Day participants, any educator can contact the AHC to request a tour and guided introduction to primary source research for their students. In addition to supporting these outreach and education activities, in 2012 the AHC reference staff assisted 2,192 researchers who visited our facility—including 749 students who visited the AHC as part of a class assignment. Additionally, there were 1,005 research requests from individuals not able to visit the AHC in person; each of these requests receives up to one hour (and, unofficially, even longer) of research assistance. Public service is clearly a strong aspect of the AHC's mission; however, we have discovered since the implementation of MPLP that there are ways in which minimal processing has changed the kinds of service that we are able to provide.

Minimal processing allows us to provide both "more" and "less" for our researchers. One of the greatest advantages of allowing research use of our minimally processed collections is that, almost immediately after a collection arrives at the AHC, it can be opened to the public. Researchers have access to the entire body of a newly acquired collection (barring any donor-imposed access restrictions). This grants scholars the opportunity to gather evidence to support original arguments and to explore novel approaches toward both innovative and more established subject matter. It enables the AHC to provide a high level of transparency about our stewardship practices; donors and researchers alike can easily see the workflow of our processes. In our redesigned MPLP workflow, user demand also plays a role in influencing additional processing. Collections are sometimes identified for additional processing only when researchers use a collection or request information about it. This allows the AHC to better marshal its limited resources toward high-priority collections that we know will be used in addition to grant-funded processing projects that specify which subject collections must receive attention.

However, there are limitations of minimal processing that impact the depth of service that we are able to provide for our researchers. Instead of using the complimentary hour of research assistance we offer all off-site patrons to locate an exact document or photograph, with minimally processed collections we may only be able to use this hour (and often additional time) to track down a possibly relevant series or general date range. We can sometimes only clarify for a patron whether the collection contains a certain type of information but are not able to confirm specific facts. We can offer duplication services at a cost, but this doesn't always satisfy researchers because of the expense or volume necessary to help them locate the information they need. For example, a researcher might end up having to request all correspondence from January to June 1931 from an individual's collection, which may amount to several hundred pages. At the same time, we typically try to limit copy and scan orders to approximately 250 pages because of the frequency of duplication requests. In instances such as these (detailed or high-volume information required but the collection's description is vague), we also commonly refer patrons to proxy researchers if we are unable to meet their needs within the time we are able to spend on their query. Both of these options—for patrons to pay for duplication of sometimes substantial bodies of records and for them to hire independent researchers—represent a distinct decrease in the level of service we are accustomed to providing for fully processed collections and certainly are a change for many of our patrons who have used some of our more detailed inventories and meticulously processed collections.

Minimal processing affects our distance patrons, but it also has a significant impact on our on-site researchers as well. Researchers may encounter large collections without inventories or, at the least, very rough box listings. These patrons are frequently scholars, graduate students, and lay researchers, but the AHC has also hosted donors-as-researchers whose collections are so massive that only an outline of what types of material are available in which boxes has been completed. While frustrating for any researcher, the experience of searching fruitlessly for one's own donated materials can be particularly aggravating. Researchers may also encounter collections in poor conditions—dusty, disintegrating, and without a clear organizational scheme. These issues are obviously inconvenient for researchers and may leave them with a negative impression of our services as archivists. Still, the opportunity to access collections that they might otherwise not have been able to use usually overwhelms any residual negative impression.

However, often the first and most pressing challenge when patrons are using minimally processed collections is pacing the retrievals of material. When it is unclear what a collection contains, researchers may need to request more material than otherwise needed to ensure that they have not missed any helpful information. And when the contents of a collection have only a vague listing, there is no telling how quickly a researcher will complete a review of each box. It could take anywhere from hours to just a minute or two for the researcher to ascertain the relevance of the box contents. This means that student assistants may be involved in a constant cycle of material retrievals, and other staff members may be called in to assist with what can be a nearly constant endeavor of retrieving and returning boxes of a collection. While these constant retrievals are taking place, other reference work is not—duplication orders are waiting, other reference requests are queued, scholarship and teaching activities are on hold while all members of the department assist with the retrieval of collection material. These departmental impacts are absorbed into the daily workflow, but indeed there are challenges, and we are conscious that this also may have a significant effect on a visiting patron's ability to successfully conduct his or her research in the time they have available on site.

Many of these challenges for us and for researchers are due to the lack of detail in minimally processed collections' inventories or the lack of any inventory at all for the collections that only have a collection-level catalog record. This lack of information is at odds with the high level of description needed to assist researchers. To address this, it was evident that departments needed to collaborate at more intensive levels. As staff across departments considered what we could do to best address this issue, what emerged was a revised workflow structure that allowed for increased flexibility in job responsibilities—often ones that crossed departmental boundaries. The resulting cross-training for members in all departments has given us all a better understanding of the needs, constraints, and optimal workflows of other departments. In turn, this enables greater efficiency in providing access to collections for our researchers.

IMPLEMENTATION

With the increasing amount of interconnected job responsibilities across departments, a broader view of reference and access services emerged. Processing archivists, in addition to monthly reference desk shifts, were performing reference work by creating collection inventories. Reference archivists were providing researchers with content lists and creating inventories for small collections. The ultimate end of these updated responsibilities focused on the needs of end users while maintaining smooth operations within the AHC's departments.

Within the processing department, one of the first changes to workflow that arose from the implementation of MPLP was the order in which collections were processed (that is, processed above and beyond the minimal description provided for all collections during accessioning). Prioritization of collections shifted from "first-in/first-processed" to giving precedence to collections with demonstrated or anticipated research use. This is one area where collaboration between the reference and processing departments became essential. Because their primary responsibilities are to serve patrons and answer reference requests, the reference

department has a keener sense of not only which collections would benefit from further processing but also *how* they would benefit from further
processing. For example, are the patrons confused with the current organization of the finding aid and it needs better intellectual organization?
Does the box listing in the current finding aid clash with the contents of
the boxes due to the discrepancies between the original inventory and
actual collection material? Are the contents of the collection interesting
and important but aren't reflected in the current finding aid? Does the
collection even have a finding aid? Input from the reference staff helps
focus processing resources on creating descriptions that promote more
efficient access to the collections, both for staff and users.

To provide a mechanism for reference staff to give this input, we
created two files on the intranet drive: one called "Wish List" and the
other called "Unprocessed Material Used by Patrons." These were recently merged into one "Wish List" document, as the distinction between the
two types of requests seemed irrelevant. Now, when members of the
reference department encounter a collection that they feel warrants reprocessing or receive a patron request for material that is in a collection
with no content list or with a minimally descriptive content list, they add
it to the list along with a brief note on why it was added in order to help
guide processing decisions. If this request was made by an on-site researcher, clearly the collection will not be reprocessed in time for their
current use, but this provides demonstrable evidence that the collection is
currently being used. If a patron contacts the reference department about
a collection with plans to visit the AHC at a later date to do research and
this collection has no content list, the collection is added to the file with a
note on when the researcher is expected to be at the AHC along with any
other notes that may be pertinent. In this instance, reference also contacts
the processing department to alert them of the impending patron arrival.

Collections on this electronic list are given processing priority. Collections are also added to the "Wish List" when other processing concerns
are present. For example, the content list does not accurately match up
with the box contents, preservation issues are identified, or the general
organization of the collection confuses patrons, among other concerns.
Collections that have high use are also added to the list if reference feels
they would simply benefit from a more detailed content list or may be
worth digitizing. These reasons and concerns are included in the electronic file as notes. When processing archivists need to start a new collection, they pull up this file and choose a collection from the list after
consulting with the head of processing. While this system still means that
users and reference staff encounter minimally processed collections that
are difficult to navigate, it does mean that we are able to more quickly
rectify the problem by moving it up in the processing queue, allowing
greater access and ease of use for future researchers.

Prior to the implementation of MPLP, all collections catalogued and searchable in the catalog had some form of finding aid or inventory. However, since 2006, all collections at the AHC have a collection-level record in our OPAC even if they lack a basic box listing. In many cases, the reference department receives inquiries and requests that pertain to collections that have only a catalog record (and no box listing). To assist patrons in using these collections, as well as ourselves, as we attempt to provide effective access to them, the reference department will occasionally provide ad-hoc folder or box listings if none already exists in connection with patron demand. These may be added to the filing cabinets of print inventories in addition to being sent to the patron. While it is too time intensive to do this for each request that pertains to collections without inventories, the department strives to provide this courtesy as patron demand and other responsibilities permit. Student assistants are regularly enlisted to assist with this task, as well. For collections that are two cubic feet or smaller, the reference department possesses the purview to generate an official inventory if none exists. However, the majority of the collections without inventories that receive attention from researchers are much larger than two cubic feet. If it is feasible, archivists may opt to generate a very quick listing to assist a researcher "on the spot," or if the collection appears to be the target of renewed research interest, it will be placed on the "Wish List" mentioned earlier. While taking staff and student time to create these lists does take us away from our regular reference duties, it is ultimately an important, initial investment in making the AHC's collections more accessible to the public for research use, as well as providing for smooth reference operations in the long term.

Another element in our effort to provide better access to minimally processed collections is changes in how materials are selected for digitization. In response to MPLP, the digital programs department, with increased collaboration with both the processing and reference departments, targets materials that would benefit from online access. Previously, material was only digitized in response to patron requests or as part of a digitization grant. Specific items were picked from collections, and metadata was added at the item level. In 2008, digitization procedures changed to accommodate MPLP. Larger sections of collections are now chosen to be scanned (folders, series, or even whole collections). Furthermore, metadata for digitized material is no longer added at the item level but at the folder level. With the exception of the file name or unique identifier, all items in a folder receive the same metadata. After implementing these changes, the amount of material digitized increased dramatically, from approximately 13,000 scans the first three years to 90,000 scans the past three years. The digital programs department also has a "Digitization Wish List" of collections or parts of collections that would benefit from digitization. Archivists in both the processing department and the reference department can add collections to this list. As collections are being processed, if processors see material they think would benefit from digitization, they add the collection and box numbers to the list. If reference archivists notice high demand for a particular collection or subject area, they, too, can add to the list. After digitization, the collection's finding aid is updated with links to the online materials so users can bypass the reference department altogether and access the materials directly. The reference department has found that instructors are using these digitized materials for class assignments, researchers have discovered relevant clusters of information through a simple web search, and photo duplication requests have been streamlined for both patrons and archivists.

RESULTS

Several examples of reference archivists working with processing archivists follow. Such collaborations have enabled the AHC to provide better service to our researchers working within the environment created by our institution's embrace of the MPLP philosophy. In several instances, reference and processing archivists collaborated in the format outlined by the new workflows we had created—additions to the "Wish List" and direct requests to the processing archivist—but other instances explored more flexible, case-by-case arrangements. These examples illustrate how encouraging cooperation between departments is necessary in an MPLP environment in order to provide researchers with the additional descriptive information they need in a timely fashion. However, we believe they also illustrate that, just as with MPLP itself, flexibility should always be the watchword.

Lester Hunt Papers

The papers of Lester Hunt, a Wyoming politician, are frequently utilized in University of Wyoming history courses. Furthermore, the collection has received frequent research use over the past year as a result of one patron researching and writing a book about his life and the sociopolitical climate of the world in which he inhabited. To investigate so closely Hunt's life and career, the researcher needed to review nearly the entire collection. While the researcher was using the collection, it was in the midst of being processed. This created the logistical need to communicate with the processing archivist working with the Hunt collection in order to locate the boxes of material currently located in the processing department and to determine which boxes were still located in regular storage areas as well as any boxes that had since been renumbered. In addition, reference archivists coordinated with instructors regarding which of the boxes (and more specifically which subject matter) might be better suited for class assignments and research projects, as the inventory would more accurately reflect the collection's contents.

This frequent and intensive use of the collection was one element in flagging it for additional and more detailed processing. The head of the processing department identified three factors that led to the reprocessing of the collection:

> The first in weight was probably the accumulated evidence of high use, along with feedback about poor condition and organization. The second point was the specific knowledge of a [particular] researcher's experience with it. That might have landed it on the Wish List. The third factor was the new accretions that had been added in 2003–2004. As a result of high historical use statistics, a specific request, and the acquisition of new material not covered by the previous finding aid, the collection was identified as a high priority.[3]

The Lester Hunt papers contained all of the standard criteria that generally recommend collections for reprocessing, and in this case they reflected the personal and professional legacy of an important Wyoming political figure as well.

University of Wyoming Agricultural Extension Records

Another example of increased interdepartmental communication and cooperation occurred with the University of Wyoming Agricultural Extension Records. The Agricultural Extension office, in celebration of its one-hundredth anniversary, determined to assemble a retrospective to honor the evolution of the department, consisting of four distinct parts: a thirty-minute video, a photo essay, a traveling exhibit, and an online display in a dedicated portion of their website. The collection had been accessioned in multiple accretions, and many of the most pertinent records had no inventories or box lists. The department hired a faculty member of the history department—a longtime researcher at the AHC— to search for relevant materials for the commemorative project. Working with the university archivist—a member of the processing department— and one of the reference archivists, the researcher acquired a crash course in processing in order to create a box-by-box listing of the collection's contents. The researcher was instructed in the preferred method of inventorying the collection—nothing was to be separated, but collection contents, if clearly out of a designated order, could be reordered. For example, annual reports of regional extension chapters could be filed in chronological order. If contents were in severe disarray, some semblance of order within that particular box could be recreated.

However, because the usual research rules continued to apply—the work took place in the AHC's public reading room—only one box was allowed to be used at a time, though multiple boxes could be used during a research visit. The reference department contact took charge of retrieving materials and coordinating with the researcher about visit dates and took receipt of the box lists to send to the university archivist. The university archivist was and is consulted with questions about inventorying procedures.

At the time of writing, the inventory produced by the proxy researcher may be used as an interim guide by other researchers using the collection. Ultimately, the inventory will be used by the processing archivist as the basis for future processing and disposition decisions, providing an invaluable resource to mapping a chaotic and disorganized collection While this is a unique partnership between the AHC and an external department as well as two internal AHC departments, it has so far proved to be an effective way to meet the needs of our researchers and the many demands on AHC staff members' time.

William Boyd Papers

One example of a collection at the AHC that has been processed more than once (at different levels each time) are the papers of William Boyd, the actor who portrayed Hopalong Cassidy. The William Boyd papers total 141 cubic feet, and it is one of the most high-profile and highly used collections at the AHC. The first round of processing many years ago resulted in a catalog record and a typed finding aid, including a fairly detailed content list. The content list, however, was only minimally organized intellectually. It was tedious to read through and not available online. At a later date, it was reprocessed, with the end result being an EAD finding aid that could be accessed online. At this point, the container list was slightly revised to have a more coherent intellectual organization, but it was mostly a rekeying of the original inventory into the new EAD format. Recently, it was reprocessed again at a much more detailed level of granularity. The reference department had identified several issues with the finding aid. Aside from insufficient intellectual organization, many items were not in the boxes specified. Because of its high use and the added burden that these insufficiencies were placing on reference, the processing department determined it was worth the time to fully reprocess the collection yet again at a more detailed level.

Reprocessing a high-use collection presents both challenges and opportunities and can require intense communication between the reference and processing departments. Like the Lester Hunt papers, while the Boyd collection was being reprocessed, more than one researcher was requesting information on the collection. One was an off-site researcher with a digitization request, and one was a researcher from Australia planning a future on-site visit. For the off-site duplication request, the fact that it was being reprocessed was very fortuitous, as one of the items requested for electronic duplication was not physically located in the listed box. If the collection had not been completely pulled for reprocessing, it would have been extremely time consuming, if not impossible, for that material to be found. As it was, the processor was able to narrow down the search to a manageable number of potential boxes the item may have been in and found the requested material in a relatively short amount of time during the typical processing workflow. Communication between the reference and processing archivists alerted the processor of the need to locate the absent but highly desired material.

The researcher planning a visit from Australia provided a different set of challenges. First, it was important for reprocessing to be completed by the time the researcher arrived on site. This gave the processor a very clear deadline, which helped inform the level of detail and reorganization that could go into the reprocessing of the collection. Second, the researcher had sent a list of items and box numbers that he would like to look through upon arrival. This demonstrated one hurdle for reprocessing a collection. Because the collection was being reorganized, some of the box numbers listed in the current finding aid were no longer accurate. Fortunately, the processor was informed of this by reference early on during reprocessing. Any box numbers that were changed that had been requested by the patron were marked down with their old and new box numbers.

The processor was also made aware of the types of materials that the patron was requesting, and this also helped inform the processor on the level of detail to use in the content list. A large portion of the collection was manufacturing files related to Hopalong Cassidy merchandising deals. The current finding aid was at the folder level, and each folder was labeled with the company name and a complete street address. Initially, the processor planned to keep the listing at the folder level and list the company name in the content list but not the address. However, the patron's request involved researching all the connections William Boyd and his enterprises had with Australia. This included all the manufacturing files that had an Australian address. Because this was a demonstrated use of this information, the processor decided to include the state and/or country where the company was located (in lieu of the complete address or total lack thereof). Being cognizant of how researchers are using a collection is extremely beneficial in determining what level of detail is needed in processing particular collections or even particular series within a collection. Collaboration and communication between reference and processing is fundamental in this respect.

Dave Garroway Papers

The reference department received a request from an off-site patron regarding materials in the papers of Dave Garroway, the original host of the *Today Show*. This seven-cubic-foot collection only had a catalog record with a very brief biography and scope and content note. There was no content list, not even at a box level. The reference archivist contacted the head of processing to inquire if any processors were free to quickly process the collection and complete a finding aid with a container list. As it happened, a processing archivist was in need of a new project. Because there was a current reference request regarding this collection, it took priority over other collections on the processing "Wish List." The processor was able to process the collection with a complete finding aid and content listing (primarily at the folder level) within two weeks, an even shorter period than is allocated for answering each reference request (thirty to sixty days).

LESSONS LEARNED

When working with minimally processed collections, the management of patron expectations becomes an important aspect of the process. Reference archivists need to clearly communicate the status of the collection in question. For example, is there a legacy finding aid available? Is the collection minimally processed with only rudimentary collection contents inventoried? Regarding the researcher's specific question, how likely is it that we will be able to locate the information that will fulfill the researcher's needs? Much of the impatience and frustration that researchers sometimes express seem to emerge from the fact that archives, for the lay researcher, remain mysterious places; our routine operations remain opaque. Researchers may assume that we know the names and dates of each and every letter in the collections under our care; there are institutions that do focus on item-level collection management that they may have worked with in the past. Providing some perspective on our day-to-day functions and the reasons behind these decisions often results in a more satisfying interaction with our collections and our archivists alike.

Communicating with our donors about expectations they may have prior to our taking receipt of a collection is also extremely important. A recent interaction with a donor-cum-researcher underscored the necessity of clear agreements about what we are able to provide by way of research assistance. A donor who remains active in his or her academic field may need to contact the reference department to obtain copies of correspondence, reports, or other key documents. However, the specificity of the request may not align with the broad strokes with which the collection has been accessioned or later processed. When individual documents are needed and the collection is quite large, reference archivists may be called to review the entire contents of the collection box by box. Typically, such a request would be referred to a proxy researcher; however for requests from a collection donor or a member of the donor family, AHC archivists try to answer these questions in house. This is an issue that could be mitigated through clear communications to our donors—collections are not processed at the item level, and the AHC has no plans to start doing so. Still, if a collection is slated for processing, a reference archivist will consult with a processing archivist to see if any requested documents have turned up or if the processing archivist might be able to identify the item during the course of their work with the collection.

CONCLUSION

With the assistance of multiple departments at the AHC, we have been able to improve the quality of research services we offer to our donors, our scholars, our university community, and other stakeholders even while maintaining an MPLP approach to processing collections and providing access to all of our collections. Communication between all departments at the AHC is not only an essential aspect of maintaining consistent service for researchers but has also contributed to the evolution of the workflows and policies regarding reference and processing work, as well as the projects in which our digital programs department is involved. In a parallel (but unrelated) effort, the AHC has made a concerted effort to increase cross-training for staff members in different departments. Yet the ad-hoc cross-training that has emerged as a result of greater fluidity between distinct positions has done more to supply different experiences and skills for AHC staff than a formal initiative. These interdepartmental skills are used when the situation requires them rather than for professional development or other purposes, which has contributed to the sustainability of informal cross-training.

In addition, we have found that interactions with researchers, donors, and the scholarly community require forthright communication from the beginning of the interaction; we have learned that we need to be clear from the start about what services we can provide our diverse researchers and donors and what we may be unable to accommodate based on the degree to which the materials in question have been processed. We've also explored creative solutions to supply donor organizations with the detailed research assistance they require while also progressing with collection processing; our experience with the University of Wyoming Agricultural Extension records is the first instance that a long-time researcher is serving a dual role as lay processor. This instance demonstrated that, with a little flexibility, we can find innovative solutions that benefit all parties involved. MPLP is a clear boon for researchers in many ways; there is no doubt about that. However, it also has costs for both researchers and reference staff. It has changed the nature of our reference services and processing work at the AHC and created some challenges. Yet, if we view these challenges through the dual lenses of flexibility and collaboration, we start to see them not as challenges but unique opportunities.

Emily Christopherson *is assistant processing archivist and* **Rachel Dreyer** *is assistant reference archivist at the American Heritage Center, University of Wyoming.*

NOTES

1. Mark Greene and Dennis Meissner, "More Product, Less Process: Revamping Traditional Archival Processing," *The American Archivist* 68, no. 2 (Fall/Winter 2005), 208–63.

2. Dennis Meissner and Mark Greene, "More Application while Less Appreciation: The Adopters and Antagonists of MPLP," *Journal of Archival Organization* 8, no. 3–4 (2010), 174–226.

3. Claudia Thompson, e-mail to Rachael Dreyer, May 3, 2013.

TWO

Managing Risk with a Virtual Reading Room

Two Born-Digital Projects

Michelle Light, University of California, Irvine

In March 2010, the University of California, Irvine, launched a site to provide online access to the papers of Richard Rorty in the form of a virtual reading room.[1] Although we didn't know it then, we quickly learned that we were one of the first academic repositories in the United States to risk providing remote, online access to born-digital manuscripts. The virtual reading room mitigated the risks involved in providing this kind of access to personal, archival materials with privacy and copyright issues by limiting the number of qualified users and by limiting the discoverability of full-text content on the open web. In January 2013, we launched a site providing access to another group of born-digital materials, the papers of Mark Poster. The two collections had as many differences as they did commonalities, and a comparison of the two projects is useful for understanding the range of decisions and issues that ultimately impact access to born-digital personal manuscript collections.

In 2006 Richard Rorty donated his papers to the University of California, Irvine, Critical Theory Archive (UCI CTA).[2] At his death in 2007, the *New York Times* hailed him as "one of the world's most influential contemporary thinkers."[3] An American philosopher, he developed a distinctive form of pragmatism and made significant contributions to literary criticism, political theory, and other scholarly fields. He was also a public intellectual, writing for such publications as *The Nation* and *The Atlantic*.

By 2009, the UCI CTA had received multiple requests to use Rorty's papers, so we made it a priority to get them processed. During processing of the approximately twenty-five linear feet of papers, archivist Dawn Schmitz discovered seventy-eight 3.5-inch floppy disks in the collection. At the time of the discovery, I, as head of special collections, archives, and digital scholarship, was also leading an initiative to implement an institutional repository that emphasized access to unique forms of faculty research output not appropriate for the University of California's eScholarship repository. We were looking for a pilot project for our local DSpace installation, and this fit. Moreover, I jumped at the opportunity to gain staff assistance and expertise throughout the libraries for working with our first born-digital collection.

Not long after we started working on the Rorty collection, however, Mark Poster contacted us about his papers. He was a professor at UC Irvine best known first for bringing French critical theory to the United States and then for theorizing about digital media, particularly the Internet. I went to his house with a lot of boxes, expecting to pack up mostly paper files, and walked away with just a few boxes and a portable hard drive that he had used to transfer the bulk of his files to us. As we worked on his born-digital papers, we were confident that we would be able to process and provide access to his papers in the same way as with the Richard Rorty papers. We were wrong.

PLANNING THE RICHARD RORTY PROJECT

In 2009, when I first learned about Rorty's floppies, I knew enough about electronic records to know that we needed to get data off the disks sooner rather than later and that we needed to take precautions to prevent accidentally altering the files. My primary motivation, however, was that researchers were asking that we make this material available as soon as possible. I looked around for information about the latest best practices and projects, but I did not find any that were scalable for a department of my size or easily implemented for a priority processing project. We did not have the expertise or resources to initiate a digital forensics lab, like the one at Stanford University, or to initiate an emulation project, like that for the Salman Rushdie papers at Emory University. We also noted that researchers had to visit reading rooms to use born-digital materials at Emory, University of Texas at Austin, and the Library of Congress. We needed to make our materials more accessible in response to remote-user demand.

I was inspired to act quickly with the limited resources at hand by three presentations I had heard years earlier. First was the encouragement by Rachel Onuf in 1999 at the Society of American Archivists' annual meeting to move beyond all the technical jargon and complicated standards and just do what you can to rescue content from floppies and move it forward. She made a compelling case for how easy it might be, with some common archival sense, to work with "electro-manuscripts."[4] Second was the James Duderstadt project at the University of Michigan in 1998, where obsolete word-processing files were converted to Word 6.0 files and made accessible in this format. Currently the files are in PDF and linked from the finding aid.[5] Third was the Norman Mailer project at the Harry Ransom Center, where archivists cataloged each file taken from floppy disks and made them accessible to researchers in DSpace, an open-source institutional repository platform.[6] Building on these ideas and projects, I planned for us to use our existing computers to read the floppies and transfer the files to a networked server, migrate the files to PDF, and describe and upload them in a batch to our DSpace repository.

Among its other features, DSpace allows you to limit access to registered users. At the Harry Ransom Center, the born-digital manuscripts in DSpace are only made accessible on site. This model may follow the restrictions set forth in the pertinent sections of the Copyright Act of 1976 (17 U.S.C. § 108 (b)).[7] However, after reviewing the gift agreement for the Richard Rorty papers, I believed the agreement allowed us to make the materials more widely available. Rorty authored almost all of the content on the floppy disks, so the rights accorded in the gift agreement covered all but a few files. The gift agreement provided that he, followed by his widow after his death, retained copyrights to the materials, including all publishing rights. The agreement also stipulated that the "material may be made available for research without restriction according to the established procedures of the UCI Libraries." What are our established procedures, and how might they apply to digital content? In a nutshell, we allow anyone to do research in our collections so long as they fill out our registration form and agree to our rules. People do not have to visit our four walls to use our material, as we regularly provide photocopies or scans of materials to distant patrons who cannot afford to visit. If we limited access to the Rorty files to our physical reading room, then we would be in the position of printing out and mailing copies of the files to remote users—that is, if we followed our existing access model. Only researchers who visited us could take advantage of the "search" capabilities inherent in born-digital material.

So I proposed that UC Irvine create a virtual reading room to mimic the model of access we provided in our physical reading room. We would allow anyone who agreed to our terms to view the materials, and they would be able to make personal copies for research purposes. I thought this would uphold the spirit of the gift agreement by making materials available according to our established procedures and also allow for in-person and remote researchers to take advantage of the scholarly potential for digital materials. I also believed that the limited online access within a virtual reading room would not infringe on Rorty's widow's rights to control the formal publishing and wide distribution of the papers. She would still retain the right to grant permission to someone to create and publish a critical edition. The key to this approach was developing an easy way to get researchers to agree to our standard terms before granting them access to the files.

In addition to copyright and the terms of the gift agreement, I was also concerned about third-party privacy. As is typical in faculty papers, I expected his files to contain letters of recommendation as well as student records. While we had to identify and remove student records, as they were protected by the Family Educational Rights and Privacy Act (FERPA), I did not see a legal reason to restrict letters about his colleagues and former students. I believed these would have scholarly value for those studying Rorty. Nevertheless, I did not think it fair to have these indexed in Google, as the person asking Rorty for a recommendation had a reasonable expectation of privacy. After a few experiments, we discovered that the files in the virtual reading room were not indexed in Google (only the metadata we supply to describe the file is). So, we planned to remove student records but leave all other correspondence in the collection.

IMPLEMENTING THE RICHARD RORTY PROJECT

In her initial survey, archivist Dawn Schmitz opened a few dozen of the digital files and compared them with the paper files we had. She found that some of the printouts in the files reflected the content of the floppies, but many of the digital files represented unique content. The files were absolutely necessary for studying Rorty's scholarly work. Researchers needed to use them in conjunction with the paper files. Indeed, when Dawn first started working on the papers, she contacted Neil Gross, who published the biography *Richard Rorty: The Making of an American Philosopher* in 2008. Gross had used the papers before they came to UC Irvine. In e-mail, he anecdotally attributed the floppy disks as one reason he ended the biography in 1980. These discoveries solidified our commitment to access.

After the files were transferred to a server, our library's information technology staff created an automated inventory of the files, resulting in a spreadsheet that listed all of the file names, their directories, the dates the files were last modified, and their checksums. This spreadsheet helped us analyze the files more effectively. With the checksums of the files, we could tell that approximately 500 of the 1,600 files were exactly the same. However, many of the files with the same names were slightly different, so we made the decision to keep all variants but to discard exact duplicates. Schmitz noted, for example, ten distinctive drafts of the manuscript "The Decline of Redemptive Truth and the Rise of a Literary Culture"; the variants showed the evolution of Rorty's thoughts.[8]

The file inventory and our appraisal decisions had implications for how we decided to present the files to users. I had initially thought that we would arrange and describe the digital collection according to each disk. Specifically, each record in DSpace would correspond to a disk and include all of the files on that disk. However, once we found and discarded so many duplicates, description of each disk no longer made sense because we altered their original contents. We also found that describing each disk did not make good intellectual sense because the content of each floppy was quite random. Rorty probably inserted whatever floppy was close at hand to save a file. However, I still was not ready to commit to item-level description. I suggested that we sort the spreadsheet and cluster together all of the files with the same name. Unfortunately, this method would have generated more work than describing each file individually. In DSpace, you can only provide one date in the "date created" field. Because we were planning to migrate the files into PDF, the original "last modified" date would no longer be associated with the migrated file; the date had to be provided separately. So, if we bundled all of the files with the same name together and presented them in DSpace, we would have had to create a separate manifest file to capture each file's original characteristics.

Most significantly, we found that bundling the files as a compound object in DSpace would have made searching for content difficult. For example, if a user was searching for a phrase and the phrase was found in a single file, the search results would bring the user a record for the compound object, not to the individual file with the search hit. If we put more than a few files in the compound object, a user would have to download each individual file and search for the phrase that resulted in the hit. Because we expected our users to look for variations in phrases in Rorty's various drafts, we believed that compound objects comprised of multiple files would not support expected patterns of use. DSpace's architecture forced us to the item level.

After deciding that item-level description was the most efficient and user-friendly option, we used the spreadsheet to structure the descriptive work. Thinking forward to access in DSpace, this meant that each file would get its own DSpace record with item-level metadata, including an individual title and its "date last modified." Researchers could then sort the files by date or title to see variants and their progression. We had the option of using the file name as the title of the document (many of Rorty's file names were eight or less characters) or creating more meaningful titles. Because this was our pilot project for DSpace and because the Rorty papers were one of our premier collections, we decided to invest effort in generating meaningful titles for each file. Schmitz opened up each and every file, perused it quickly, and gave it a DACS-inspired title (see figure 2.1). She provided concise, accurate titles at the rate of approximately two to three minutes per item.

Item-level review also gave us assurance that we would not inadvertently provide access to a student record. Unfortunately, we did not have a foolproof means to tell if Rorty was writing a letter about a current or

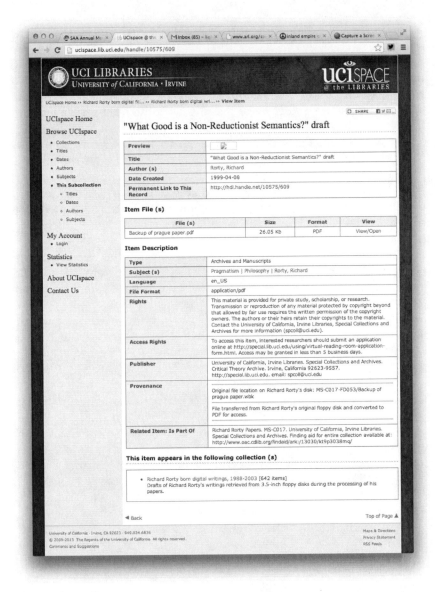

Figure 2.1.   Example of a record from the Rorty Collection in DSpace.

former student other than by analyzing the tense of his verbs. If Rorty wrote a letter about a student in the present tense, we removed the page from the PDF file (Rorty often kept all his correspondence in one big file) and inserted a page describing the restriction. We did not restrict letters of recommendation for former students and colleagues, however. Schmitz reassured me that Rorty was pretty positive about all of his colleagues, so it was unlikely anyone would be upset about seeing his or her letter of recommendation in the files.

The next piece was getting researchers access to the files. In order to create the virtual reading room, we needed researchers to agree to our terms of use and then for the libraries' IT staff to add researchers' e-mail addresses to the list of users authorized to view and download the files. We could not find via DSpace a way to automate this process, so we launched the collection with a low-tech option. We had researchers print out our standard reading room application form, sign it, then fax or e-mail it back to us. After special collections staff received it, we filled out a work ticket to request that our libraries' IT staff add the user to the authorized list. Users would then be able to create an account in DSpace and log in to use the Rorty materials.

We contacted Mary Rorty, Rorty's widow, to let her know that we planned to make the materials available. She gained access to the virtual reading room and praised the ability to have remote access to this previously unknown content. She liked our solution because the content is not too discoverable, in case she or her children decide to publish a critical edition of unpublished manuscripts, but it still facilitates scholarly research about Rorty by scholars.

We then went live in March 2010. We allowed OCLC to harvest all of the DSpace records for inclusion in WorldCat. We sent out press releases to let UC Irvine and Rorty scholars know about the availability of the papers. We were surprised by the enthusiastic responses.

RESULTS OF THE RICHARD RORTY PROJECT

A few days after we sent out the press release, we were contacted by UC Irvine professor Liz Losh about organizing a symposium in honor of the Richard Rorty archive. Held on May 14, 2010, at UC Irvine, the symposium featured seventeen speakers from around the country, including Rorty scholars, archivists, and digital humanities faculty.[9] Two of our hypotheses were confirmed. First, the Rorty scholars appreciated having searchable, remote access to the digital files. In fact, a few researchers developed their papers around discoveries found from searching for terms and names in the files. The researchers also used the files long before they came to Irvine to see the papers. Second, the scholars found that the files went hand in hand with the papers; one could not be studied without the other.

The Rorty scholars followed our procedures for gaining access to the virtual reading room without complaint or problem. However, during the symposium, Christine Borgman, professor and presidential chair in Information Studies at UCLA, roundly criticized our archaic method for granting access. She highlighted the analog portions of our reading room application, especially how we reminded our researchers to lock up their bags and pens before using the reading room. She missed our point that we were trying to demonstrate that access to the virtual reading room was granted according to our "established procedures." We were nervous at first about the virtual reading room and wanted to make sure we could justify it in terms of our gift agreement.

As time wore on and more and more people used the virtual reading room without incident, we streamlined the application process to make it less cumbersome for our users. We created a webform [10] to capture user information and provided a check box where users could indicate agreement with the terms for use (see figure 2.2). [11]

We also created new rules for the virtual reading room specifically. The conditions for use are:

- For purposes of research, teaching, and private study, users may reproduce (print or download) any item in accordance with the principles of fair use (U.S. copyright law) or link to materials from this website without prior permission on the condition they give proper credit to the UCI Libraries.
- Materials may not be used for any commercial purpose without prior written permission from the copyright owner.
- Materials may not be republished in print or electronic form without prior written permission from the copyright owner and/or the UCI Libraries.
- Materials may not be mounted on an additional server for public use, including use by a set of subscribers, without prior written permission from the copyright owner.

Between April 2010 and July 2013, the files have been viewed 4,883 times. More than forty people have registered to view the materials, about half of them interested archivists and the other half serious scholarly researchers interested in Richard Rorty. The success of the project contributed to the permanent addition of a digital projects specialist to the libraries' IT, with a focus on supporting special collections' acquisition and management of born-digital materials. The Rorty project also established an important pattern of collaboration between information technology staff and archivists at UCI.

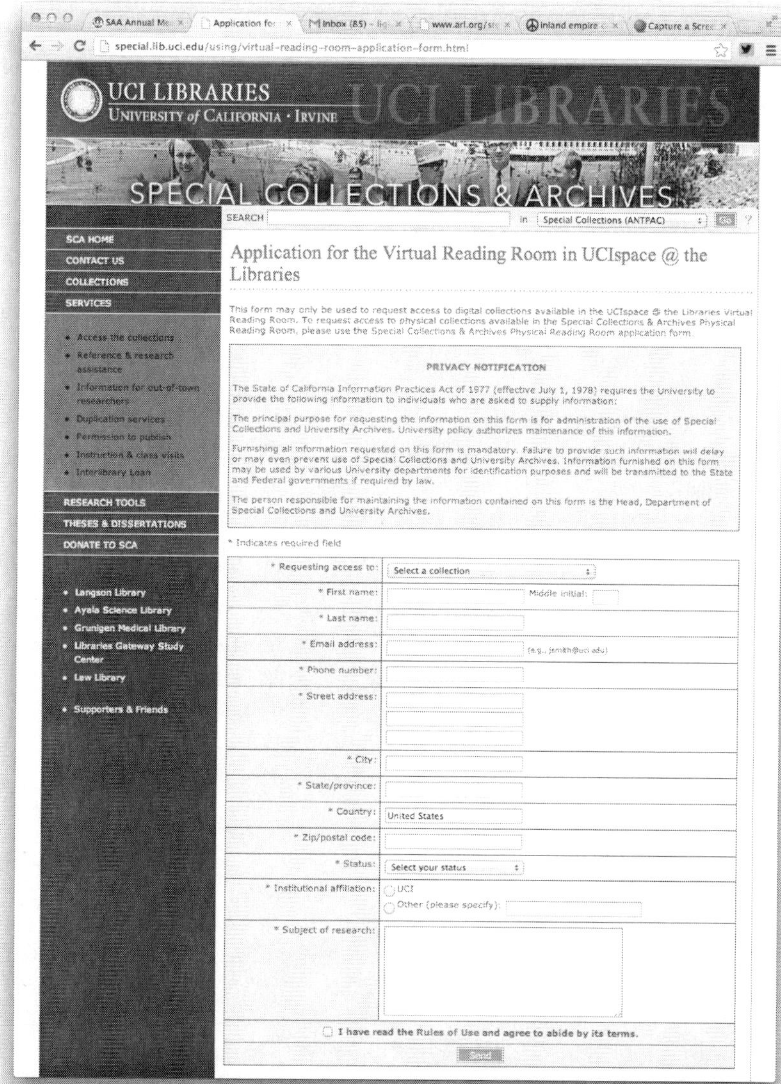

Figure 2.2.   The web-based application for access to the virtual reading room.

PLANNING THE MARK POSTER PAPERS PROJECT

The Mark Poster papers proved very different in terms of processing and access.[12] The Rorty papers were a paper–digital hybrid collection; the Poster papers were almost exclusively digital. Mark Poster wanted his entire collection made available online. He asked that we insert a Creative Commons License into his gift agreement to make his intentions clear. Whereas the Rorty born-digital files were almost exclusively written by Rorty and were all word-processed documents, the Poster papers included not only e-mail, writings, and lectures but also materials authored, and in some cases previously published, by others. There were Listserv conversations, papers from others e-mailed to Poster for comment, PDFs of published articles, images collected for research, and so on. The collection was just as diverse as you might find in a typical faculty paper collection in the analog environment. Unfortunately, Mark Poster died in 2012 before we had the opportunity to discuss with him how we would have to limit access to copyrighted content in his papers and that his Creative Commons License could not be extended to every item in his files.

In planning the project, we outlined very similar workflows and goals as with the Rorty project. We planned to migrate most of the files to PDF when possible, host content with privacy or copyright issues in the virtual reading room, and provide access to the materials in DSpace at the item level. Moreover, we hoped to isolate files authored exclusively by Poster and make them available openly outside of the virtual reading room. Fortunately, Poster had organized his files into very distinct series. Unlike the random order of the files on the Rorty disks, the original order of Poster's files had discernible meaning. There were four times as many files as in the Rorty project, however, so we knew we had to find efficiencies in processing them. In order to provide item-level access to the files with a minimum amount of effort, we planned to experiment with automating the description of the files. We hoped that, by looking at the first one hundred characters of each file, we could generate titles automatically without having to review them first.

Much of this project did not proceed as planned.

IMPLEMENTING THE MARK POSTER PROJECT

Despite our hopes that we could automate description of the files, the plan didn't work. The first one hundred characters of each file were largely gibberish; the characters were from the file headers, not from the user-provided content. In reviewing the automated inventory, we decided that the existing file names were not descriptive enough to help a user decide whether to open the file. We went back to the Rorty model and decided to review each file individually to give it a descriptive title.

At the time of the project, the University of California system was in the middle of budget cuts and a hiring freeze. Without any permanent archivists on staff, we tapped UC Irvine's critical theory librarian in hopes that his subject expertise would expedite item-level description.

He completed two series. The "Mark Poster administrative records for the Critical Theory Institute" was placed in the virtual reading room because it contained correspondence authored by others. The "Mark Poster lectures" are openly available, as Poster was the sole author. However, when we moved on to the larger series, we quickly realized that the pace for item-level description was not sustainable with our staffing situation. Moreover, the contents of the next series were unexpected. When the critical theory librarian had to take on additional duties elsewhere in the libraries, we assigned an intern to the project, but the issues proved too complex, and the project languished.

Significantly, we discovered that Poster did not author the bulk of the files in some series. For example, we found a number of unannotated published articles, drafts of articles submitted to him for peer review, and copied Listserv conversations. There were original articles and notes by Poster within the files, but it was often impossible to tell the difference between his Word files and those authored by others. We thought about identifying all of Poster's original work and just providing access to them, but the files' existing metadata did not help us, so we could not make that determination with certainty. We also did not believe that the research value of the series warranted item-level description or appraisal of every file. We would have spent more time looking at files for removing them rather than adding value to Poster's own work. However, the presence of these collected files also added value to understanding Poster's work because he obviously collected and organized them in relation to his own writings and lectures. They could be analyzed to understand the evolution of Poster's thought. We decided to keep almost everything and look for ways to provide access to them in a way that would be in keeping with our limited staffing resources and also reduce our risk for copyright violation. There were three turning points for the project in 2011–2012.

First, we saw what the University of Michigan was doing with delivering born-digital material in their DSpace repository. They were using DSpace to deliver an entire series or subseries of personal papers, for example the Peter Pollack papers, where they provided a zip file with about five hundred megabytes of project files.[13] The disadvantage of this method is that the contents of the zip file are not searchable within DSpace. In order to search, you have to download the zip file and do the search on your local computer. Furthermore, you have to download the file before you know exactly what is inside. But there are big advantages as well. Foremost, you quickly deliver content with very minimal metadata work or analysis. Also, you make it difficult to find and use copyrighted content. It is doubtful that anyone would find and download this file in order to get access specifically to a copyrighted item. In other words, there would be no economic harm to copyright owners if a library or archive redistributed copyrighted content within this context. In this case, almost certainly only someone interested in Ann Arbor or Peter Pollack would download this file to see what is inside.

Second, the Association of Research Libraries (ARL) *Code of Best Practices in Fair Use for Academic and Research Libraries* was published in January 2012, and this gave us confidence to proceed with the protections offered by the virtual reading room and DSpace's limitations for surfacing content within zip files.[14] The ARL code applies fair-use analysis to library-specific situations. It explains that "judges generally refer to four types of considerations mentioned in Section 107 of the Copyright Act: the nature of the use, the nature of the work used, the extent of the use, and its economic effect (the so-called 'four factors')."[15] There were two ARL principles that applied to the Poster project. First, for preserving at-risk items, it proposed, "It is fair use to make digital copies of collection items that are likely to deteriorate, or that exist only in difficult-to-access formats, for purposes of preservation, and to make those copies available as surrogates for fragile or otherwise inaccessible materials."[16] For these materials, the ARL code encouraged institutions to limit access to "authenticated members of a library's patron community, e.g., students, faculty, staff, affiliated scholars, and other accredited users." Our virtual reading room procedures accounted for this. However, the ARL code also suggested that we not make copies available when a "fully equivalent digital copy is commercially available at a reasonable cost" and that we make "full attribution" to all items available online. For the reasons mentioned earlier, we could not invest this level of effort and analysis in making these materials available.

However, the next fair use principle applied to creating digital collections of archival and special collections materials. The ARL code proposed, "It is fair use to create digital versions of a library's special collections and archives and to make these versions electronically accessible in appropriate contexts."[17] It recognizes that the research value of the collection resides in the "unique assemblage or aggregation" rather than in the individual items. Presenting these unique collections in their entirety "can be highly transformative." It cautions libraries against providing access to materials available commercially but encourages libraries to allow copyright owners to register their objections, take technological steps to prevent downloading and reuse, and make collections available in their entirety to strengthen fair use arguments. The ARL code is focused on digitization, not on born-digital materials, so more thinking could still be done about the application of fair use to born-digital materials.

Third, UC Irvine hired a metadata librarian in the cataloging department to focus on digital projects. At first, the differences in theoretical traditions and practices between catalogers, who focus on item-level description and subject analysis, and archivists, who focus on levels of description, summary analysis of related materials, and provenance, were very apparent. The learning curve for both of us was large, and we invested more time in creating high-quality, item-level description than anticipated.

In the end, however, we found a way to deliver aggregates of related items that achieved a balance of user convenience, efficient processing, and risk mitigation. We used zip files to deliver Poster's directories to users, so users could download the files to their own computers and search their contents (see figure 2.3). Although we migrated most of the files to PDF, we preserved Poster's directory structure and file names. The zip files are accompanied by spreadsheets that describe the contents of each zip file (see figure 2.4). For some of these zip files, we provided item-level titles for each file.[18] For zip files with lesser research value, we did not provide descriptive titles but just listed the files' original names and "last modified" dates. The spreadsheet is searchable in DSpace, so this promotes discovery. The contents of the zip files are not searchable in DSpace.

We decided to put the most problematic directories, "Notes" and "Publications," which included copyrighted material that might be available commercially, in the virtual reading room. Again, the virtual reading room requires users to fill out a user application and accept our rules and warnings about copyright. It also prevents Internet search engines from indexing the contents of the files (only the metadata we provide is indexed). These barriers to access prevent the Mark Poster papers from becoming an alternative source to commercially available content. Only researchers interested in Mark Poster would accidentally discover copyrighted content as they look through the materials Poster used in creating his writings. When discovered, the files have a transformed meaning in relation to the larger aggregate of Poster's research interests.

Is this legal? Technically it probably isn't, but we can make good arguments that we are following research libraries' best practices for fair use. The virtual reading room protects UC Irvine in four important ways:

1. It shows that our intent is to provide access for educational, personal, or research purposes only, just like we have always done for similar analog materials in our reading room.
2. It makes use of the material conditional upon users agreeing to only use the material for educational, personal, or research purposes.
3. It limits the discoverability of private or copyrighted content to those individuals who are specifically interested in studying specialized topics.
4. It shifts accountability for violating fair use to the user.

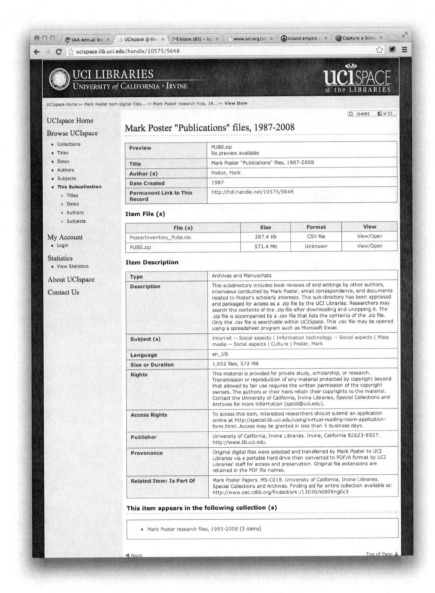

Figure 2.3.   An example of a DSpace record for over 1,900 files in Poster's "Publications" directory.

RESULTS OF THE MARK POSTER PROJECT

We released the site in January 2013, just before I left my position at UC Irvine. Between January and July 2013, the Mark Poster papers had 1,025 views. Because many of the files are openly available, we do not know as

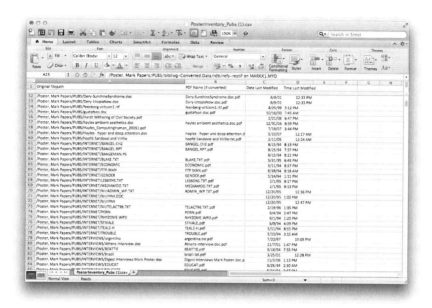

Figure 2.4. An example of the accompanying spreadsheet with more information about the package of files.

much about who is using the materials and why. I expect that many of these users are curious archivists.

I have received criticism from other librarians and archivists about the barriers to access with the virtual reading room, but my response is that these barriers have enabled access. I have also been asked about whether we talked to our university's counsel before proceeding. No, we did not check with them. UC Irvine's library administration was comfortable enough with our methods and explanations to allow us to proceed with launching the collection. I realize that other institutions may have different relationships with their university counsel, and this additional step may be warranted.

LESSONS LEARNED

These projects resulted in many lessons learned, both big and small. We learned that processing decisions for born-digital collections can and should be guided by the needs of the end user, particularly in thinking about how to deliver content to end users remotely. Just as in the paper environment, born-digital materials will only fulfill their potential research value insofar as they are usable and used. However, even though we constantly held the end user in mind, many of our decisions were the result of DSpace's features and limitations and our limited resources when dealing with legacy technologies.

We learned by doing and probably made multiple missteps in how we treated the original digital files. We learned, for example, that we need to take more care when rescuing content from legacy media to protect the original content. We also learned that the rapidly changing digital environment in which our record creators operate adds to the complexity of managing this material. Papers rescued from floppy disks have very different issues than papers transferred from hard drives. After 2000, humanities faculty are likely to have far more diverse content in their files, including databases, spreadsheets, images, videos, e-mail, HTML, and so on. As they interact with more individuals and communities online, and as they gather their research online, issues relating to appraisal, preservation, authorship, ownership, and copyright become more complex.

We also learned that collaboration is essential. These projects were made possible only with the help of multiple departments within our libraries, including special collections, information technology, monographic cataloging, collection development, and web services. We also had assistance from our campus IT in hosting DSpace and from the California Digital Library in hosting the preservation masters in the Merritt Repository. I also learned that archivists remain essential to these projects because of their training and expertise in understanding provenance, context, aggregation, authenticity, and efficiency.

It is also no surprise that we found item-level description not to be sustainable even though users might appreciate it. As Mark Greene and Dennis Meissner exclaimed, "good processing is done with a shovel, not with tweezers."[19] Archivists must find efficient ways to appraise, arrange, describe, and provide access to born-digital materials at higher levels of control.

But most significantly, we learned that you need to be flexible. As we were forging into new territory, we often needed to change our plans and thinking in response to new discoveries about the nature of the files, the limitations of our technological systems, and staffing issues.

CONCLUSION

I am proud of the risks we took at UC Irvine to make this material available online, albeit with restrictions, in the virtual reading room, and I hope that it will inspire other institutions to consider the issues and experiment with options for remote online access as well. While I may no longer speak to what UC Irvine may do in the future, I will say that there are many possibilities for how to organize, present, and deliver this material, and there are also many options for protecting privacy and copyright interests. I would like to see more institutions try different approaches so we may eventually identify best practices for discovery and access. While there is some consensus that we may take risks in digitizing and delivering archival collections,[20] it is unclear to me whether these practices and laws apply to born-digital materials. Hence, I would like to see more engagement with copyright and privacy laws as they might pertain to born-digital archival collections.

I am concerned that, as a profession, we might be building more "hidden collections" as we accept born-digital collections but lack practices and systems to make them widely available. Moreover, I am sometimes concerned that developing best practices for ingesting born-digital materials is growing too fastidious and resource intensive at the expense of access rather than following trends in the analog archival environment for letting go of perfection to make the materials available in less-than-perfect states so researchers may have access to them more quickly. While not to discount the technical expertise needed to ingest and preserve archival materials properly so they may be authentic and perpetually accessible, we must now also focus on access in the here and now.

A 2012 ARL survey of research libraries found great variation in how the sixty-four respondents provided access to born-digital materials: "Two-thirds of respondents provide online access to a digital repository system. Just under half provide in-library access on a dedicated workstation. Users who bring their PCs to 22 of the responding libraries can access born-digital materials stored on portable media. Eighteen respondents (28%) use third-party systems such as CONTENTdm, Archive-It, Dropbox, and YouTube to share materials with researchers."[21] Half of the respondents indicated that the biggest challenge to providing access to born-digital materials are "concerns about copyright, confidentiality, privacy, intellectual property, and personally identifiable information."[22] The report notes how our profession lacks an automated system that will negotiate complex access restrictions with our users. This should sound familiar. Nevertheless, the report lauds the shift from a "wait-and-see attitude to a more empowered something-is-better-than-nothing approach to managing born-digital materials." Despite the fact that "enterprise-level systems and best practices for managing these materials in an archival setting are still in development,"[23] many research libraries just like UC Irvine are taking risks and experimenting with managing and delivering access responsibly to born-digital materials. I encourage you to do so, too.

Michelle Light *is director of special collections at the University of Nevada, Las Vegas, University Libraries. Between October 2008 and February 2013, she was head of special collections, archives, and digital scholarship at the University of California, Irvine, Libraries.*

NOTES

1. The "Richard Rorty born digital files, 1988–2003," *UCI Libraries*, are available at http://ucispace.lib.uci.edu/handle/10575/7. Accessed January 28, 2014. The finding aid for the entire collection is available at "Guide to the Richard Rorty Papers MS.C.017," *Online Archive of California*, http://www.oac.cdlib.org/findaid/ark:/13030/kt9p3038mq. Accessed January 28, 2014.

2. The Critical Theory Archive is part of the UCI Libraries special collections and archives department. In 2009–2010, when this project was under way, special collections and archives had five, then four, full-time staff. It is a medium-sized department, managing approximately five thousand linear feet of archival material.

3. Patricia Cohen, "Richard Rorty, Philosopher, Dies at 75," *New York Times*, June 11, 2007, www.nytimes.com/2007/06/11/obituaries/11rorty.html?_r=0.

4. Rachel Onuf, "Electro-Manuscripts and the Historical Records Repository" (paper, Society of American Archivists annual meeting, Pittsburgh, PA, 1999).

5. "Digital Documents 1986–1997" in the "James J. Duderstadt Papers 1963–1997," *Bentley Historical Library, University of Michigan*, accessed July 21, 2013, http://quod.lib.umich.edu/b/bhlead/umich-bhl-9811?byte=143088926;focusrgn=C01;subview=standard;view=reslist. The project is described by Nancy Deromedi, "Case 1: Accessing, Processing, and Making Available a Born-Digital Personal Records Collection at the University of Michigan," *Millennium Project* (University of Michigan) October 25, 2006, accessed July 21, 2013, www.bentley.umich.edu/academic/practicum/2008/digital_cases/case1.pdf.

6. Gabriela Redwine, "An Acquisitions Narrative: The Practical and Theoretical Challenges Presented by Norman Mailer's Electronic Records" (paper, Society of American Archivists annual meeting, San Francisco, CA, 2008).

7. 17 U.S.C. § 108 (b) states: "The rights of reproduction and distribution under this section apply to three copies or phonorecords of an unpublished work duplicated solely for purposes of preservation and security or for deposit for research use in another library or archives of the type described by clause (2) of subsection (a), if— (1) the copy or phonorecord reproduced is currently in the collections of the library or archives; and (2) any such copy or phonorecord that is reproduced in digital format is not otherwise distributed in that format and is not made available to the public in that format outside the premises of the library or archives." Although whether this applies to born-digital unpublished works is debatable.

8. Dawn Schmitz, "The Born-Digital Manuscript as Cultural Form and Intellectual Record," *eScholarship: University of California*, (paper, Irvine, CA, May 14, 2010), www.escholarship.org/uc/item/5ss5696t.

9. Some of the papers may be found at "'Time Will Tell, But Epistemology Won't: In Memory of Richard Rorty': A Symposium to Celebrate Richard Rorty's Archive," *eScholarship: University of California*, at www.escholarship.org/uc/uci_libs_rorty. Accessed January 28, 2014.

10. See "Application for the Virtual Reading Room in UCIspace @ the Libraries," *UCI Libraries: Special Collections and Archives*, http://special.lib.uci.edu/using/virtual-reading-room-application-form.html. Accessed January 28, 2014.

11. See "Rules of Use for the Virtual Reading Room in UCIspace @ the Libraries," *UCI Libraries: Special Collections and Archives*, http://special.lib.uci.edu/using/docs/rules-of-use-virtual-reading-room-ucispace.pdf. Accessed January 28, 2014.

12. The Mark Poster born-digital files are available at http://ucispace.lib.uci.edu/handle/10575/1336. Accessed January 28, 2014.

13. For example, see the "Ann Arbor Projects," *Deep Blue*, 2012, in the Peter Pollack digital materials series, http://deepblue.lib.umich.edu/handle/2027.42/89903. For this series, the finding aid (located outside of the DSpace repository) describes the folders that are inside each zip file and also provides a more descriptive path for access and can be found at http://quod.lib.umich.edu/b/bhlead/umich-bhl-

2011178?byte=7225273;focusrgn=C01;subview=standard;view=reslist (accessed July 21, 2013).

14. Association of Research Libraries, *Code of Best Practices in Fair Use for Academic and Research Libraries,* January 2012, www.arl.org/storage/documents/publications/code-of-best-practices-fair-use.pdf.

15. Ibid., p. 7.

16. Ibid., p. 18.

17. Ibid., p. 19.

18. See, for example, the files in the Mark Poster Book Drafts series at http://ucispace.lib.uci.edu/handle/10575/1337/browse?type=title. Accessed January 28, 2014.

19. Mark A. Greene and Dennis Meissner, "More Product, Less Process: Revamping Traditional Archival Processing," *The American Archivist* 68, no. 2, (Fall/Winter 2005), 240, http://archivists.metapress.com/content/c741823776k65863/fulltext.pdf.

20. For example, see "Well-Intentioned Practice for Putting Digitized Collections of Unpublished Materials Online," *OCLC,* May 28, 2010, accessed July 21, 2013, www.oclc.org/content/dam/research/activities/rights/practice.pdf; or Laura Clark Brown, Judy Ruttenberg, and Kevin L. Smith, J.D., "The Triangle Research Libraries Network's Intellectual Property Rights Strategy for Digitization of Modern Manuscript Collections and Archival Record Groups," *Triangle Research Libraries Network,* January 2011, www.trln.org/IPRights.pdf.

21. Naomi L. Nelson, Seth Shaw, Nancy Deromedi, Michael Shallcross, Cynthia Ghering, Lisa Schmidt, Michelle Belden, Jackie R. Esposito, Ben Goldman, and Tim Pyatt, "SPEC Kit 329: Managing Born-Digital Special Collections and Archival Materials," *Association of Research Libraries,* August 2012, 14, http://publications.arl.org/Managing-Born-Digital-Special-Collections-and-Archival-Materials-SPEC-Kit-329.

22. Ibid., p. 15.

23. Ibid., p. 18.

THREE

Improvements on a Shoestring

Changing Reference Systems and Processes

Jackie Couture and Deborah Whalen, Eastern Kentucky University

When you work in a small archives, the thought of making improvements to reference services may seem like a daunting task given the price tag on some of the exciting new products available, the time limits of archives staff, and the lack of technology expertise. On the other hand, how do you *not* make improvements? So maybe the question should be how *can* you make improvements with limited funds and limited outside expertise? In our experience with changing our reference systems and processes, we found that it is possible to make improvements with basically no investment of money and using our existing resources. Driven by technology and researcher expectations, we were able to creatively make use of a planned website migration to implement much-needed updates to our reference services.

When Eastern Kentucky University, a regional, coeducational public university with an enrollment of about 16,000 students, began migrating its static HTML webpages to Drupal in fall 2011, the special collections and archives department had the opportunity to get our own subdomain (archives.eku.edu) and to organize our own content. This gave us the flexibility to expand user access to our reference services and to improve our reference processes. For example, before the Drupal implementation, our only way to receive electronic reference requests was through e-mail. However, with hundreds of static HTML pages on our website, we needed to limit the inclusion of our e-mail contact information to only a few selected pages, making it difficult for researchers to ask questions and submit requests.

Like any library or archives, we receive requests for information daily. Our requests come from students, faculty, and administrators, as well as the general public. Requests from the general public come from all over the United States, with occasional requests from other countries. Some of these requests are brief, to the point, or relatively quick to resolve. We term these as *ready reference* because they usually involve us answering questions from researchers immediately or referring them to an appropriate source that they can review for themselves. These interactions will most often occur in person, over the phone, or through online chat, but they may happen through e-mail or snail mail, and we do not charge for this service.

When requests move beyond ready reference to those that require us to do extensive research for a person, we call these *research requests*. These are most likely received through e-mail or by letter, and we do charge for these services. We also charge for what we call *duplication requests* from those who want copies of images, videos, manuscripts, or other materials in our collection. When we began to explore the larger topic of improving our reference processes, we decided that ready reference questions were not an issue but that we needed to address procedures, forms, and fees for research and duplication requests. The actual process of answering ready reference and research requests was not changed, only the way we communicated with researchers.

For years, we had no set procedures for responding to research and duplication requests. A request would arrive in the form of a letter, and library staff or a volunteer would do the research and mail copies of the findings. We rarely charged for research or copies. If no one was available to respond to a request immediately, it sat in a folder. Eventually that folder turned into a box of requests waiting to be answered. No one kept statistics on how many requests we received, and no one knew who was taking care of a particular request. This was especially problematic when irritated researchers would call to ask about the status of their requests. In 2002, we formalized the process for requests, created a form for people to use to request research and copies, began logging the requests, established a six-week response time, and began charging a fee for our services.

While these improvements helped in 2002, by 2011 we realized that we could improve the process even further by implementing new technologies to improve ways to request reference services from our website. We used EKU's switch to the Drupal content management system for its website as a driver for making the wide variety of changes we knew we needed to make.

PLANNING

The planning process for the new website and improved reference services involved the entire special collections and archives staff. We are a small institution with a diverse collection of oral histories, film and video, books, manuscripts, and university records staffed by three full-time professionals and several student workers. During 2012, we also had a part-time staff member who happened to be working on his master's degree in library and information science from the University of Kentucky.

One of the first things we did in the planning process was to gather information. We went to workshops, participated in a vendor demonstration, and reviewed other archival websites for content and research procedures, looking for ways to improve our own online presence. We looked specifically at reference processes for other archives and how they used their websites to communicate with users. This research, along with the experiences, gave us a foundation to begin work.

Our first concern in redesigning our web presence was improving the ways people located information about us and our collections. We knew that the presentation of our finding aids was integral to the experience that researchers had using our website and finding information they needed. Because our finding aids were on static webpages with no standardized format, we looked at both Archon and Archivists' Toolkit to better manage them. Both are content management systems designed specifically to manage archival materials. We attended workshops on both platforms sponsored by the Kentucky Council on Archives Content Management Working Group. These workshops consisted of the Society of American Archivists webinars on the platforms and presentations by Kentucky archivists using each software package. After careful consideration, we decided that the public interface of Archon would serve our needs better, and we received approval from the library's information technology department to proceed.

Choosing Archon also allowed us to provide additional ways for people to contact us with reference requests. This interface gave researchers better and easier access to collections, as well as the ability to schedule reference appointments or e-mail reference questions directly from any point in the finding aid database, greatly improving the ability for researchers to ask questions. The public interface of Archon would also allow us to easily add digital content resulting from duplication requests to begin building an online digital collection. In addition, we found that the Drupal template being provided for our use included our contact information on every page. We also considered providing an instant reference service from our website using a webchat service called LibraryH3lp. This was an easy decision because our library was already using it to answer reference questions directly from its website in real time.

After planning for better access to our finding aids and providing more ways to contact us, we began to discuss improving procedures for our reference process, which included keeping better statistics, tracking requests, and delivering materials. Although we already logged the number of requests received by researcher type (students, faculty/staff, or the general public) and question source (e-mail, phone, letter, and in person), we weren't tracking the number of items digitized. With the importance placed on digitization efforts in the library, we felt it was necessary to provide library leadership with this information. We decided that a simple form in Google Docs would give us an easy way to record the number and type of materials digitized by researcher type.

In regard to the delivery of materials, we decided to go all digital when completing requests. For years we had been scanning photographs on demand and providing only digitized versions. We decided to expand this practice to other archival materials, giving us the opportunity to build our digital collections. We planned to scan materials only once, providing the digital copy to the patron as well as attaching the digital derivative to the finding aid in Archon. This would have the added benefit of reducing the handling of fragile manuscript materials because they would be available online for future researchers. To ensure efficiency, we planned to scan materials at the level of description. For example, we would scan single items only when the collection was described at the item level or the entire folder would be scanned for those items described at the folder level. This procedure would be more efficient because it would reduce confusion regarding what items had previously been digitized and would allow us to make use of descriptive metadata. Going all digital meant we had to improve our delivery method, so we considered YouSendIt and Dropbox. Even though both services offer free and paid versions, we found that Dropbox offered a way to increase our storage space without additional cost.

In conjunction with these changes to our reference procedures, we began to discuss using webforms for research and duplication requests. We looked at several approaches before making a decision. Early in the process, we considered using Google Docs to create an online form for research requests. This form would be submitted, and the fee would be calculated and communicated back to the researcher, who would then mail a check to cover the cost of research. Other areas of the library were already using Google Docs effectively for collecting reference and instruction statistics and book recommendations. This would have been an easy, free solution to simplify the reference process and to make sure researchers paid the correct fee for services in advance. On the other end of the price spectrum, we considered Aeon and participated in their online demonstration. Aeon would give us the ability to allow researchers to create accounts through which they could request materials, schedule research appointments, ask reference questions, and request duplication of materials. We were impressed with the product and felt it would solve a lot of our issues, but our library budget would not support the annual maintenance fee. In the end, we chose to use Drupal because, as we learned more about its capabilities, we realized that we could use it to create the forms that we needed as easily as we could in Google Docs. Using Drupal was also an advantage because it was supported campus-wide and the university maintained user accounts with access permissions.

As we developed the request forms and the new reference procedures, we also discussed revising our pricing structure. We realized that the biggest problem we had with the pricing structure involved requests for copies of family files, which are composed of a variety of genealogical information compiled by archives staff and researchers about local families. Although these files are most often found in public libraries, there was not a public library in our community until 1988, and we had always served as the local genealogical repository. The pricing structure problem arose because we used one form that was created in 2002 for several types of requests, including lookups of single items, copies of family files, and hourly research. Because each of these had different fee structures, researchers rarely sent the correct fee for the service they requested. The index to 640 family files was already published on our website with page counts, so we decided that the easiest solution would be to publish specific prices for each file. Published prices, combined with a shopping-cart approach for family file requests, was our initial idea. Unfortunately, university-supported online payment options were not available, so we could not pursue this option, which would have streamlined the process, eliminating the need for a researcher to mail a payment. Instead, we planned to create a separate webform in Drupal for family file requests.

Once we developed a plan for handling the family file pricing, we realized that the fees for our other reference services were not an issue and decided to make no further changes. We did, however, realize that our decision to go all digital when completing requests meant that we needed to set fees for digitizing manuscripts and other text-based materials. To ensure that the new digital process was well received by researchers, we made this fee the same as the cost of photocopies. While we still planned to provide photocopies on request, we would now charge an additional fee for that service.

As we mentioned earlier, we decided to make digitized manuscript materials available to the public online after the first duplication request. However, we decided not to make digitized family files freely available online because fees for these requests represent a significant income source for our archives. From family file requests alone, we receive more than one thousand dollars per year, and these funds are used to support archival activities.

From the beginning of the planning process, when we gathered information and weighed alternatives, to the point of making decisions, the special collections and archives staff worked together to determine how to resolve the issues we had with online access to reference services and our reference processes. For easier access to information on our website, we agreed to use Archon, Drupal, and LibraryH3lp. To improve our reference processes in terms of procedures, forms, and fees, we planned to keep statistics with Google Docs, to deliver all requested materials digitally through Dropbox, and to use Drupal webforms for requests, creating a separate webform for family file requests (see table 3.1).

IMPLEMENTATION

Once we made the decisions about what we wanted to change and how, we started acquiring the software necessary to achieve our goals. The software components of this project required no cash outlay because they were either already in use, open source, or free cloud-based products. There were, however, staff costs associated with the implementation of each of the technical components, as well as the nontechnical ones. The time of the entire special collections and archives staff was devoted to this project for about a year. Although this caused other archival projects to be put on hold, our staff greatly benefitted by learning the processes as we developed them, eliminating the need for formal staff training.

Requests Received Using	Requests Tracked Using	Requests Completed Using	Statistics Reported Using
Chat • LibraryH3lp	Not Applicable	• Completed in LibraryH3lp	• Logged in Library Stats
Letter (Postal Service) • Printed Family File PDF Form • General correspondence	Paper System	• Digital content delivered via Dropbox, if applicable • Hardcopy content delivered via postal service, if applicable	• Logged in Library Stats • Logged in Google Docs Digitization Form, if applicable
Email • Archon Web Form • Drupal Contact Us Form • Drupal Duplication Request Form • Drupal Research Request Form • Omeka Web Form	Outlook System	• Digital content delivered via Dropbox, if applicable • Hardcopy content delivered via postal service, if applicable	• Logged in Library Stats • Logged in Google Docs Digitization Form, if applicable

Table 3.1 New systems mapped to the reference process

Implementing Archon required the involvement of the university's information technology department, which created the web database necessary for the Archon installation, and the library's system administrator, who installed the Archon software. The special collections and archives staff was then responsible for the configuration and migration of legacy data. Daniel Weddington, our part-time staff person, completed this configuration as part of his "Professional Fieldwork Experience" course through the University of Kentucky's School of Library and Information Science. He studied the software and, with our input, personalized the settings for our institution, allowing researchers to contact us from any page in the finding aid database. He also added accession records, which was a fairly quick process as we only needed to copy our accession database to a spreadsheet, map the fields in our database to the fields in Archon, and import the spreadsheet. Adding collection content was another story. It took us more than six hundred hours to convert flat HTML and PDF finding aids to spreadsheets that could be uploaded to Archon. Even though it was labor intensive, this process allowed us to standardize our finding aids and provided a much easier way to search our collections and respond to reference requests.

Like Archon, Drupal is an open-source content management system; however its purpose is website development. EKU had already begun using Drupal on campus, and the university's web team set up the special collections and archives development site. They also programmed special features of the site and modified the appearance as necessary. As we designed the front page of our website, we had the web programmers include a search box for the Archon database so that researchers could search manuscript materials from the main webpage and easily access the Archon interface. One strength of Drupal is the ability to add blocks of content throughout a website, making it easy to add a "contact us" link and phone number on every page. This link opens a simple form that allows researchers to e-mail us with questions.

We also used blocks to implement the webchat service LibraryH3lp. The service was already in use in other library departments, and we asked the library information technology staff to create a queue for archives, as well as accounts for each staff member in archives. We then created a block with the code for the chat widget and placed a chat box on every page of the website, allowing patrons to get answers to reference questions directly from the website in real time. If no staff members were logged in to chat, the e-mail address would show up in the chat box. Just recently the chat service was upgraded to allow queues that were not logged in to roll over to the main reference queue. This provided archives researchers access to the chat service outside our normal operating hours, and questions that the reference staff cannot answer are forwarded to archives in the form of an e-mail. Because LibraryH3lp was already in use in our library, the time and expense to expand the service to archives was minimal.

After the implementation of online access to reference information and staff through Archon, Drupal, and LibraryH3lp, we looked at changing our reference processes. We wanted to create a workflow that would allow us to receive all reference requests by e-mail and to deliver all materials online. Drupal included a module specifically for making webforms that could be set up to be submitted directly to the archives e-mail account. We used this tool to recreate our duplication request form, a family file request form, and our research request form. In order to simplify the research request form, we modified it to handle only in-depth requests that take a significant amount of time and effort. After receiving a research request, we would review it, quote a fee based on the hourly rate, and fill it after we received payment.

Now that we were receiving requests through e-mail via the Drupal webforms, we moved forward with the implementation of the online delivery of requested materials. Setting up online delivery took a matter of minutes to download and install the Dropbox software, which placed a folder in Windows Explorer that synchronized automatically with Dropbox. We could then share these folders with researchers, enabling them to easily access the materials they requested. This significantly reduced turnaround times for requests, making it possible for researchers to have the materials they requested within a day or two of receipt of their order and payment.

The final component of the process that we needed to put into place was collecting statistics and tracking the status of the requests. Tracking was important because multiple staff members worked with requests, and we needed to be able to refer follow-up inquiries to the appropriate person. We decided that we needed to log statistics in two places after a request was completed. The first was driven by library policy and the second by the need for digitization statistics. While we were revising our reference procedures, our library started using Library Stats for recording reference transactions and statistics. Library Stats allowed us to continue to track all transactions by researcher type and question source. This system also allowed us to track time spent on a transaction and to record the questions and answers, enabling us to build a knowledge base. By fully recording the answer to the questions and adding links to relevant materials, we could use this database to easily answer repeat questions at a later date. We can use the data recorded in Library Stats to generate a variety of statistical reports. Unfortunately this system was not flexible enough to track digitization statistics. Therefore, we used Google Docs to create a form to collect data documenting the number of digitized items we provide to researchers. On this form we tracked the researcher type (student, faculty/staff, or general public), the material type, and the total number of items digitized for each duplication request.

We also wanted to document each step of the reference process on all research and duplication requests, whether received through letter or e-mail. To accomplish this, we used the request itself as a tracking tool. For request forms that we received in the mail, we marked the form with the date of receipt, the payment amount, and the name of the staff person assigned to complete the request. Once the request was completed, the date and method of delivery were noted and statistics were logged in the appropriate places. Usually research requests are logged only in Library Stats, as there is no digitization statistic to record. To capture the same information about e-mail requests, we used the color-coded categories in Microsoft Outlook. With a simple mouse click, we indicated the payment status and who the request was assigned to. After the request was completed, the delivery method was selected and statistics were logged.

RESULTS

We evaluated the results of the implementation of our plan for improving online reference services and our reference processes through feedback from the special collections and archives staff and users, as well as an assessment of the success of the project. Because everyone on staff had experience working with research requests and were aware of the problems, we had complete buy-in for improving our processes. The entire special collections and archives staff was involved in the planning and implementation stages, and we all had input into creating the new forms and revising the procedures. Likewise, we were all aware of the processes that were implemented but didn't work as planned. The processes still aren't perfect, but we are making minor adjustments as needed. From the standpoint of users, it appears that they are getting what they need in a timely manner. For example, one pleased patron recently wrote a letter to the president praising our efficiency in providing him a copy of a commencement program.

This feedback was great for providing anecdotal evidence, but we also wanted to do some quantitative assessments based on the statistics we collected. During fiscal year 2012–2013, we conducted seventy-eight chat sessions through LibraryH3lp. We feel that this number is a good start for this new service. During the same time period, twenty-six researchers e-mailed us through Archon to set up reference appointments, ask questions, or request digitization of our materials, and we received eighty-seven e-mail requests through the Drupal website. When combined with other e-mail reference transactions, we had a total of 238, which represented a 54 percent increase from the previous year. Interestingly enough, our phone reference transactions decreased by 42 percent from the previous year, and requests received by letter remained virtually unchanged.

Based on the digitization statistics form in Google Docs, we digitized 4,645 items or pages and delivered them electronically through Dropbox during the fiscal year 2012–2013. These digital objects were in various formats, including images, audiovisual materials, and text-based materials. These numbers represent a significant increase to our digital collections library, allowing future researchers to access many of these materials online. According to Google Analytics, our digital content in Archon was accessed more than 2,100 times from October 2012, when analytics were enabled, through June 2013.

The final measure that we considered in the analysis of our success was our turnaround time for answering research and duplication requests. Ready reference questions are usually answered the same day and are not included in these statistics. A random sampling of requests from 2009 to 2012 indicated that we completed them in an average of 7.1 days. In comparison, an analysis of requests during 2012 to 2013 revealed that our average turnaround time for all research and duplication requests was 4.2 days. We believe this improvement was due, in part, to the fact that Dropbox delivery is easier and quicker than mailing a letter and the new forms lead to more accurate payments. Further analysis of the numbers from 2012 to 2013 shows that 9 percent of all requests were research requests, which were completed in an average of 6.9 days. Duplication requests were completed in an average of 3.9 days. This difference was not surprising, as duplication requests are easier to delegate to student workers than research requests, which are more complicated.

By creatively adapting the systems already being used in our library (Drupal, LibraryH3lp, Library Stats), we were able to meet our needs with no additional funds. We kept our revenue streams intact and even expanded them by making family files easier to request. Ultimately these changes will reduce the time to complete requests, freeing up staff time to address other archival issues. The improved workflows also sped up responsiveness to user requests, expanded our digital offerings, and improved user access to information about collections. We accomplished all this while using tools that were free and commonly available.

LESSONS LEARNED

Maybe we should have been more intimidated when we started out to redesign so many of our processes and implement new systems at the same time, but in retrospect perhaps our small staff, limited budget, and our other constraints were actually an advantage. We weren't in a position to hire outside consultants to give us advice, and we knew we couldn't afford most of the commercial systems. All of us knew our processes inside and out, and we all agreed on what needed improvement. Although we considered many options, often what we found was that the simplest solution was the best. For example, reverting from a family file request webform back to a printable PDF resolved the issues that arose from the lack of an online payment system. We also learned not to be afraid to tackle a lot at once.

As with any major project, we made adjustments to forms and processes throughout the implementation period to achieve the results we wanted. But the only aspect of the plan we had to completely rethink was the family file online request form. Our idea was to create a form that would allow researchers to select multiple surnames from a drop-down list and would calculate the total cost of the order. The researcher would then submit the form electronically and would mail the appropriate payment. However, this didn't work for two reasons. First, researchers could only select one file at a time, and the list was so long that it was unwieldy and nearly impossible to use. Second, there was no way to duplicate a shopping cart experience, and the lack of an online payment system made the process awkward. Requests could be submitted online, but a check had to be mailed separately to complete the transaction. After a short time, we realized that this form was not working, and we replaced it with a PDF form linked to the family history file index with individual file prices. Researchers would print the form, fill it out with the files they wanted, and mail it with a check based on the published prices. While it initially seemed like a step backward, it has worked well, and we have not received an incorrect payment since we revised the process.

We also found that it was important to keep statistics to document what types of materials were being digitized and who they were being digitized for. By tracking these numbers, we can create charts to give us visual representations of our digitization efforts. Over a period of time, we made slight modifications to a very simple digitization statistics form. These changes came about as we expanded the types of materials we were digitizing and as we noticed gaps in the data. Some changes were also made as a result of inconsistencies in how the data were entered. Those inconsistencies made us realize that we needed additional fields to better capture relevant data. Keeping reference statistics gave us an assessment tool to measure the results of improved contact information on our website.

It was important throughout the process to be flexible and to be able to recognize when we were going in the wrong direction. We also found that it was very obvious when a process did not work as we envisioned in the planning stages, and at that point we had to determine which parts were not working and why they didn't work. Only then could we make changes to improve the process. Keeping our systems simple and low tech have also allowed us to have more direct control over modifying them, so that as we find areas that need improvement, we're often able to quickly make those changes ourselves. We all know that improving our processes will be an iterative activity as we find new ways to improve and the systems we have access to change and evolve.

CONCLUSION

While we are very satisfied with the results we've seen from our changes so far, we've also been surprised by the added benefit of creating a knowledge base in Library Stats to help answer repeat questions. We are especially pleased with the growth of our digital collections. Because we don't have a large staff, we aren't able to do mass digitization projects, and making digitization a part of the reference process allows us to build a digital library without extra staff. By keeping the cost reasonable, we have found that researchers are more than happy to pay for digital copies of materials. Ultimately, this process will result in fewer requests for copies, which will free up our time for other activities, such as processing and outreach. For example, after we digitized materials from the Kentucky High School Athletic Association records, our most popular collection, research questions relating to those materials dropped dramatically.

There are still several things we would like to implement to continue to improve user access to our reference services. While we have a chat box on most pages of the main website, we haven't added the widget to our secondary sites. We feel that it would be helpful to have chat available in Archon as well as our Omeka digital library sites to give researchers at those sites access to instant reference services. In the future we would also like to provide training in archival reference to other library staff so that they are better equipped to respond to chats and other questions about archival resources outside our normal hours.

We would also like to create a series of short video tutorials that would show researchers how to access materials and make requests. We have several different databases to search materials, and giving patrons a virtual tour of the website would help them find these materials more easily. We could also create tutorials to explain the request process and how to fill out the forms. Other departments in the library have used video tutorials very effectively, and we feel that they would help archives researchers find the information they are looking for more easily.

In conjunction with these additional improvements, we would like to be more proactive in marketing the services we provide. Our library has an advancement office that works to create materials for promotion and outreach throughout the library, and we need to work closely with them to develop a marketing plan for our archives.

Besides continuing to improve user access, we want to offer patrons an online payment option. Researchers are beginning to ask for online payments more frequently, and when the university implements a campuswide system, we will switch the PDF forms back to a webform with a payment option. This will work especially well for family file requests and duplication requests. Research requests will still need to be mediated, but offering an online payment option will speed up the process for those who want to pay electronically.

Another area that needs to be improved upon is tracking. As we were compiling statistics, we noticed inconsistencies in how this data was recorded. To ensure that the data will allow us to effectively assess our activities, we need to develop some guidelines for collecting statistics. A page added to our procedures manual outlining terminology to use and how to record the appropriate data will help improve this part of the process. Library Stats, where reference questions are recorded, has a place to record the time spent on each question (zero to nine minutes, ten to twenty minutes, and more than twenty minutes). We don't feel that these categories are sufficient to represent the time we spend on research requests, and we would like to expand the options to include additional ranges of time. Another useful assessment tool we would like to implement is a survey of customer satisfaction with the reference process. We also need to compile and analyze the Google Analytics data from the various websites we maintain in order to better assess the impact of our digital collections.

Overall, the changes we have made in our reference systems and processes have been positive. We had known for several years that these needed improvement; however, to implement changes, we had to make this a priority and invest the necessary time. Reference today depends heavily on technology, and being aware of emerging technologies helped us enhance our services to researchers. We found that ideas generated from other archives could be creatively adapted to fit our needs with free or low-cost technology. These, along with systems that were already being utilized in our library and on our campus, allowed us to make major improvements on a shoestring budget.

*Jackie **Couture** is manuscript curator/digital projects archivist and **Deborah Whalen** is special collections librarian at Eastern Kentucky University.*

FOUR

Twenty-First-Century Security in a Twentieth-Century Space

Reviewing, Revising, and Implementing New Security Practices in the Reading Room

Elizabeth Chase, Gabrielle M. Dudley, and Sara Logue, Emory University

Over the past year, the general public has become increasingly aware of a problem archivists have been cognizant of, and guarding against, for decades: the theft of archival materials. The case of presidential historian Barry Landau drew significant media coverage in 2012 in outlets ranging from the *Baltimore Sun* to CBS's *60 Minutes*.[1] As archivists know, this is not a new problem nor is it the case that all thefts are on par with Landau's. Still, with some exceptions, it is extremely difficult to predict what might be susceptible to theft. Ultimately our responsibility is to strike a balance between ideal security practices, real spaces, and researcher access.

We have found this especially difficult but perhaps even more important now, when archives such as our own have grown substantially in collections and patrons but not necessarily in space or staff. The Manuscript, Archives, and Rare Book Library (MARBL) at Emory University has experienced significant growth over the past decade: We have added five staff positions as well as two-year fellowships for recent library school graduates. However, our public spaces remain largely unchanged from the building's opening in 1969. MARBL occupies the ninth and tenth floors of a building shared with the general Emory Library, Goizueta Business Library, and various additional library programs. On the tenth floor, we have a balcony and exhibition area, both of which are open to the general public.

In 2002, MARBL hosted 646 unique researchers, who made 1,352 visits to our reading room. By the 2011–2012 academic year, that number rose to 1,189 researchers and 2,300 visits. We have also invested significant time and effort in developing a vibrant instruction program, which marks a shift in the dominant types of researchers we see in our reading room. Staff and faculty instructors hosted 1,357 students in 2011–2012 during 138 instruction sessions. Many of these students then comprised the 35 percent of undergraduate researchers who returned to our reading room to complete assignments and undertake independent research.

While we have grown in terms of staff, users, and collections over the past five years, many of our procedures for staffing and providing security in the reading room had not changed greatly prior to this project. The reading room consists of nine tables, six large and three small, each seating one researcher. We also have two kiosks: one for born-digital and another for audiovisual material. The reading room is monitored by two staff members: The first sits at a security desk with a networked computer. The second staffs a reference desk adjacent to the reading room entrance to assist patrons with all necessary paperwork and any reference questions; this staff member also has cameras to aid in visibility of the reading room and other secure areas. There is a door from the reading room into a staff work area and an open doorway through which patrons access the room. Lockers are located outside the reading room. Figure 4.1 is a view of our reading room from behind the security desk. Patrons enter the reading room from the left-hand side of the image.

PLANNING

While we were aware that our security procedures required review simply based on the length of time since they were last assessed and updated, there were a number of factors that pushed us to act more quickly than we originally intended. The initial driver was a planned facilities renovation of our public spaces, which will likely commence in mid-2014. We felt evaluating our processes and practices prior to renovation would enable us to address our most significant space and security needs in our updated facilities. A second factor was an internal audit, which was required by the university's development program as the result of the large donation of the Lovett Robinson Crusoe Collection; the audit began during the spring 2012 semester.

The internal audit was not originally sparked by security concerns or plans to revise our security procedures. Research services could have chosen to remain separate from this process, contributing as required but

Figure 4.1.   View into the reading room from the security desk. *Photo by Sara Logue*

not taking ownership of any specific pieces of the review. Originally we did not plan to participate heavily in the process, as the audit pertained only to procedures for collection acquisition. Then, in June 2012, it turned into a much larger process when we discovered that material from one of our collections was missing. At this time, a larger audit process took shape, and we seized the opportunity to have the outside reviewer examine all of our security procedures.

While any theft is of great concern for an institution, we believe after a thorough analysis of our materials that the missing items constituted a very small portion of one collection. We conducted a review of our records to determine who had used the collection in the preceding months. Because the materials came from a small but frequently used collection, we were able to determine approximately when they had gone missing and identify a possible culprit. We then compiled information and delivered it to the Emory Police Department, who began a formal investigation that is still ongoing. At the same time, once we had turned over all pertinent information, MARBL's research services team began an internal review of our security procedures and requested broader participation in the internal audit. Our meetings with the auditor allowed us to gain a fresh point of view and to combine that feedback with our own internal observations in order to revise our daily operations.

Once we decided that updating security policies and revising process-es in the reading room was a priority for research services, the team, including Elizabeth Chase, coordinator for research services; Sara Logue, research and public services archivist; Kathy Shoemaker, research ser-vices associate archivist; and Gabrielle Dudley, research library fellow for reference and instruction, had many discussions through the rest of the summer regarding changes to our security policies and guidelines at our biweekly team meetings.

Assessing our current reading room and security policies and then amending them to be more on par with special collection libraries at Emory's peer institutions and with the guidelines set forth by profession-al best practices was a key component of the revision process. We asked Gabrielle to conduct an initial review of the literature on security in spe-cial collection libraries in the past five years, create a survey on current security practices at peer institutions, and talk with various staff mem-bers from MARBL and the general library about security. The literature review was conducted over a three-week period and used by Elizabeth to begin team discussions. As the group discussed the literature review, we also shared information gathered from workshops and conferences we had attended, such as the annual SAA meeting, that could inform the new policies.

These conversations reinforced two key requirements for our institu-tion: (1) the need for an electronic reading room management system, such as Aeon, which would allow us to move away from copious paper records and to instead electronically store, search, and review patron use records if necessary; and (2) the need for a shared institutional policy related to security that would document the relationship between MARBL and the preexisting Emory Libraries security team to ensure that we were being consistent in our reviewing and reporting of missing ma-terials going forward.

Next, Gabrielle conducted a review of policies available via the web-sites of MARBL's peer institutions, including their reading room rules and instruction/class session practices. At the conclusion of the fact-find-ing project, she compiled a list of self-assessment questions and tips for special collection libraries to consider when revising or updating their security practices, using suggestions and recommendations extracted from the literature. In preparation for a series of team meetings, Elizabeth highlighted the four most pertinent self-assessment questions:

1. Does MARBL photocopy and retain patron identification?
2. What is the key information staff hope to glean from reference interviews?
3. Does MARBL have an articulated security philosophy with related policies and training sessions for all staff?
4. What are MARBL's goals for our safety and security guidelines?

Our discussion around these four questions, as well as the results from assessing peer institutions, most informed the policies and procedures that we ultimately implemented.

Operating as we were in the immediate aftermath of discovering a theft, the team clearly thought that some policies needed to go into effect immediately—that is, during the summer, before the start of the new school year. However, there was consensus that the majority of the changes would go into effect at the beginning of the fiscal year in September. When this time came, all patrons were greeted with a "Happy New Year" sign to remind them to complete new researcher applications; collecting new registration forms presented us with the perfect opportunity to update patrons regarding our new policies.

IMPLEMENTATION

For many years, when researchers arrived in MARBL for the first time or at the beginning of the university year, they signed our daily log, completed an annual researcher form, and showed photo ID. (In subsequent visits, they only needed to sign the log.) They then requested that materials be pulled by filling out a call slip for each book or a request form for boxes and other materials from our manuscript collections and university archives materials. However, many of our researchers have little interaction with staff at the desk, as they have e-mailed ahead with their materials requests. Researchers are asked to place personal items in a locker, with a few exceptions, as discussed later. Once seated in the reading room, a researcher's cart of materials is parked near his or her table, and the researcher is able to retrieve each box from the cart as needed. At the end of our research, discussions, and data collection, we had a list of seven key changes to these practices we felt would bring us in line with best practices and provide better overall security for our collections.

At this juncture, we realized, we had to consider how the new procedures would impact our budget as well as our staff's time. Because we were responding to an incident, we felt pressure to move quickly and so had skipped an initial assessment of the impact of our changes on our budget and staff time. We recommend that you take both into consideration during the planning process, well ahead of implementation. Thankfully for us, while a number of the changes we implemented had a financial impact on MARBL, the cost was not excessive, and we decided the expense was reasonable in order to offer as much security as we could in our current space. The key changes we implemented included:

1. adding an undergraduate page position as a third person seated in or near the reading room area,
2. scanning all photo IDs and registration forms to a secure server,

3. eliminating personal notebooks and notepaper in the reading room,
4. providing matboard for patrons photographing materials,
5. restricting graduate student workers' access to the vault,
6. establishing a library security officer, and
7. implementing proximity card access to all secure spaces on our newly renovated floor.

Adding an Undergraduate Page Position

We chose to hire undergraduate student pages to cost-effectively give us an extra level of security in the form of a third person. The page also pulls materials, thus allowing the two staff members on duty to remain at the reference and security desks without interruption. The page also checks materials as they are returned by patrons, eliminating another distraction for the two other monitors. We assessed our student staffing budget and determined that we would be able to hire two pages. We initially set out with a plan to hire and train students to work in four-hour time blocks in the reading room. We set up a table at the front of the room as their post and instructed them on the importance of keeping a watchful eye on the room when researchers were present. We also gave them full training on retrieving materials for patrons and began to implement new ways of checking in materials. This included reviewing each box to ensure that the order of the folders was correct, that none of the folders was empty, and that items were generally in place.

To inform staff, we went over the new role of the page in a biweekly staff meeting; this coincided with our rollout of all additional security changes in September. We then hired the pages in mid-October. Initially, we wanted pages to play a significant role in security and asked that, if there were researchers present, they not do other work. However, if the room was empty, schoolwork or reading was permissible. As tertiary security, the page provided a backup for the reference desk attendant and for security desk attendant, whose primary role is to monitor the room and offer clarification on proper usage and handling when necessary. As an undergraduate employee, the page was not expected to engage patrons regarding handling concerns. The page was instructed to inform a staff member at either the security desk or the reference desk, who would approach the patron and resolve the issue. We made an effort to respect the undergraduate position and to avoid putting students in an unnecessarily uncomfortable position by asking them to address handling rules with their peers or professors.

When the reading room was empty or slow, the page was also given projects that included photocopying patron orders, counting statistics, and reshelving.

Scanning All Photo IDs and Registration Forms to a Secure Server

Scanning photo IDs and adding them to a secure server gave us the opportunity to save a patron's identification in the event we needed to reference it in the future. We found that, in the case of the theft we experienced, because we had only an address and phone number that proved false (provided by the thief in the daily log), we did not have the ideal information to turn over to the police pursuing the case. Also, scanning the registration form allowed us to eliminate having confidential patron information on easily accessed paperwork at the reference desk.

We purchased a small desk scanner that allows us to feed through both the registration form as well as a photo ID. In the case of passports or other items that will not go through, we simply take the extra time to scan them on the photocopy/scanner/fax machine in the office. Once the items are scanned, they automatically create a PDF document that we save on a secure internal server. The physical registration forms are put into a folder and checked against the digital copies to make sure all were captured correctly at the end of the week. After this, the paper form is shredded and recycled.

Eliminating Personal Notebooks and Notepaper in the Reading Room

MARBL's collections, while spanning a large portion of history, include many twentieth-century materials. As such, we felt there was the potential to mistake the documents that comprise our collections for a patron's personal notes or papers. We implemented a "no-outside-paper-or-notebooks" policy to eliminate the possibility of materials mixing in with patron documents, deliberately or accidentally. We began supplying green paper in the reading room for patrons' notes. We also photocopy patron materials onto green paper if they have notes or other materials they would like to use while doing research. While this is an added expense for MARBL, it seems a small one in the name of security and researcher satisfaction.

Also implemented around this time was a "no-outside-books" policy, which we quickly amended once we determined that we could securely allow for outside books if they were checked thoroughly upon entry and exit of the reading room. We realized the hard practice of "no outside books" had a negative impact on researchers' ability to compare draft and published editions of literary materials in particular.

Providing Matboard for Patrons Photographing Materials

Previously we gave patrons folders to use underneath materials they were photographing to isolate the item in order to get a better image. The difficulty with this practice was that it gave patrons an empty folder at their desk that they could easily mix into a box. Also, it was hard for staff to tell if patrons only had one folder of materials at a time in front of them. To replace the folders, we had our conservation department cut down grey acid-free board used for making boxes. This was another small but effective change.

Restricting Graduate Student Workers' Access to the Vault

Perhaps the most difficult change for our student staff was that previously graduate student workers had access to the two vaults located within the stacks of MARBL. In an effort to limit the amount of people accessing these highly valuable materials, we eliminated all student access. Also, we implemented a vault code change policy; codes now change every six months unless staff turnover requires it to happen earlier. Inventorying the vault at regular intervals has also been added to the tasks of the rare book librarian. Because only staff is allowed in the vault, this requires some added staff time to pull materials for instruction sessions or other researcher needs, but so far this has been minimal.

Establishing a Library Security Officer

Based on recommendations from multiple sources, we established a library security officer (LSO) to provide staff with one person who could be the main point of contact for security situations. At the time of implementation, this role went to Elizabeth, as the coordinator of research services. Since then a new associate director for the library has been hired, and the role of the LSO has been transferred to this position. This is a better placement for the LSO position because certain security situations require a broader reach than research services and the associate director oversees most of the departments in MARBL. The coordinator of research services continues to play a large role in security and supports the associate director in the role of LSO. While a number of security issues stem from the reading room or patrons, there are also some issues, such as student access to staff space, that span multiple departments. We also felt it was important to place this responsibility outside any one department in case there is ever a security issue that involves staff rather than patrons.

Implementing Proximity Card Access to All Secure Spaces on Our Newly Renovated Floor

MARBL's security questions also involve multiple floors, which was another complicating factor for us. Renovations begun in early 2012 extended MARBL's books and technical footprint to include both the ninth and tenth floors. As we were contemplating changes in our security, we had not yet opened the new ninth floor spaces for use, so issues concerning security between the two floors were very much on our agenda. Coincidentally, in the spring of 2013, library security began to discontinue the use of keys and move to full use of proximity cards. These cards allow for tracking of who is walking through secure spaces and further limit access. Through these cards, then, we had the opportunity to put limitations on access by students or non-MARBL library staff and to have a record of who has been moving through secure library doors. While access to space was already limited to primarily MARBL staff, some general library staff had informal access to the space when working with MARBL staff members. We have restricted access to ensure there is a MARBL staff person accompanying any general library staff. Furthermore, use of the proximity cards enables us to determine specifically which staff or students have accessed a secure space if there is ever a question regarding our collections.

RESULTS

Change is difficult, especially when that change is sudden and requires more of both researchers and staff. We recognized the challenges involved and were deliberate about how information was disseminated both to staff and patrons. As soon as our new policies were available during August 2012, they were introduced to the entire MARBL staff. During a regular MARBL staff meeting, Elizabeth outlined the updated security policy and the rationale for the changes taking place; MARBL staff were aware of the incident of theft, but staff in the general library were not, which made some transitions difficult for those who did not yet have the full background to understand our purpose. This was especially difficult to convey, as some of the changes, such as a ban on outside paper of any kind in the reading room, were immediate, while other changes, such as prohibiting outside books, would not take place until the beginning of the fiscal year in September. While staff understood why the changes needed to be made, this did not necessarily mean that they welcomed them. Following the staff meeting, Elizabeth sent a detailed e-mail outlining the immediate changes to the reading room policies. Staff were encouraged to read over the policy and submit any questions or concerns to research services.

A critical component of the dissemination of information was a clear articulation of staff's responsibilities during their time at the security and reference desks. One of the immediate changes was the ban on notebooks. This restriction may seem simple and straightforward but actually caused a serious change in the way patrons could conduct their research. What if a long-time researcher kept all her notes about the boxes and folders she needed to consult in her favorite notepad, which now could not be taken into the reading room? What happens if a researcher was just in the reading room one week prior and could take in his research folder? In an attempt to provide the best level of service possible, staff could, at their discretion, photocopy notes for patrons who seemed unhappy or unaware of this new and sudden change in policy. We encouraged all staff to explain that, because so much of MARBL's manuscript collections are contemporary, it was difficult to distinguish our material from a researcher's notes, hence the need for the introduction of colored paper.

As more changes began to occur with the new fiscal year, so began the questions from patrons and other library staff about the sudden modifications of policies. We were initially instructed by the Emory Police Department not to speak about the theft, which complicated our communications in some ways. We have now been given approval to discuss the incident and feel that being open about our loss, especially with peer institutions, is important. However, at the time of the initial changes, we were met with a number of questions that were challenging for us to answer. Whether or not we could discuss the theft, we knew that a shared narrative among staff reinforcing professional best practices and MARBL's governing principle and goals was essential for an overall understanding of why policies had to be revised.

When fielding questions we encouraged staff to tell researchers that the new policies enable us to comply with professional best practices and best protect our materials for future use. For most researchers this explanation suffices, but for others, usually long-term or returning researchers, this is a much more difficult concept to grasp. This may change once Emory releases a statement about the theft we experienced. We will likely field questions about the theft from those researchers closely aligned with the special collections field, but the incident will not form part of our standard discussion with all researchers. We hope that, in the future, if all staff use the same narrative consistently with patrons, we will be able to keep our conversations positive and teach patrons about security.

Similarly, while it took time for patrons to adjust to the changes, it took staff just as much time. In all fairness, the new procedures added to the list of things staff not only needed to remember at the reference and security desks but also increased what they were required to do. For many staff members, desk shifts meant that they could get caught up on e-mails or other tasks; our changes significantly reduced their ability to multitask at the desk. With the implementation of the new policies, staff at the reference desk now not only have to review the annual research applications but also scan a patron's photographic identification. Additionally, while explaining which items are allowed in the reading room, staff must articulate the principles governing the policy changes and answer any lingering questions patrons may have. The staff on the security desk not only have to pay attention to the care and handling of materials but also make sure that prohibited items, such as laptop cases, notebooks, and jackets hanging on the back of the patron's chair, are cleared from the reading room. As an added layer of security, staff must also ask patrons for permission to look inside any laptops and flip through their colored papers and outside books when they exit the reading room. Undoubtedly, these procedures prompt patrons to ask even more questions, which once again demand more time and require staff to convey the shared narrative in a positive manner.

We recognized that many of our policy changes made sense in theory but had some challenges in practice. It was clear from the beginning that the policies would require assessment to determine their effectiveness.

LESSONS LEARNED

Now that we have finished an academic year with most of the new procedures in place, we have a better sense of what is working and what is not.

We believe the purchase and implementation of our scanner was a success. It was also fairly easy to implement, as the scanner we chose is user friendly and the scans save directly in the secure folder, where they will remain in accordance with our records retention policy. To date, we have not had any issues with patrons who are concerned about our request to capture their identification.

Utilizing green paper instead of allowing outside notes still meets with resistance on occasion from our patrons. We try to make everyone aware of all of our policies prior to their arrival, both through our e-mail contact with patrons and by adding our new procedures to the MARBL website, but sometimes we do not have any interaction with patrons before they come in to do research, and this rule can be a surprise to some. We try to be very accommodating about making copies of notes onto colored paper, and we continue to express the narrative of MARBL's goals and principles. It has made it much easier for us to assess, at a glance, what a patron is doing at his or her table. Implementations such as this make securing the reading room much easier when it is full or when there is a lot of other activity in the reference area.

Implementation of the proximity cards was not very smooth. There was some miscommunication between MARBL and security about our requirements. We also had unexpected difficulties communicating with our student employees. While we diligently sent out e-mails explaining changes as they were implemented, we found that students were not reading them. Also, our communication to staff about the proximity card changes was not always clear, and therefore the correct information was not making it from supervisors to students. In addition, in some cases we had to have the university issue new ID cards to students who had received their ID cards before the proximity cards were in use. This also added a cost to MARBL, as we paid for any student ID that needed to be changed. Ultimately, we were able to change all of the student cards and get them acclimated to the new system. It was not without its grumbles, but all seems to be going smoothly at this point.

While we do believe that most of the decisions we made were successful, the implementation and staff buy-in of each change has not always been consistent. For several reasons, whether it be inconsistent distribution of explanations regarding the changes, short desk shifts that hinder new policies from becoming routine, or a misunderstanding about one's responsibilities, we are looking to reevaluate how we communicate with staff and how staff is then held accountable for incorporating the changes into their desk routines.

The main portion of our new program that requires assessment is our page process. We found staff buy-in to the program was fairly low, in part due to a lack of communication from research services about the goals and intentions of the program. While we distributed information about page responsibilities at the start of the program, there was limited overall training for staff and students, so many staff members did not rely on pages, and therefore the pages were unsure of their responsibilities. We are currently assessing this program to determine whether it is one that will be maintained in the current space, reinstated in the new space, or discontinued.

Finally, we proposed a new system for tracking the status of any materials reported missing. In the reading room, when researchers notice something that is incorrect in our finding aids, we provide them with a "finding aid revision form" that is given to the arrangement and description team. We also ask patrons to complete this form if they feel items are out of order or missing. After our revision of the reading room procedures, we proposed that, any time this form indicated a missing item, it would be directed to the coordinator for research services, who would then enlist the help of the research services team to check all folders in the box and all other reasonable collection locations for the missing item. In the vast majority of cases, the item was misfiled by a user and is returned to its proper location by staff. If an item is not located, the LSO is notified, and the coordinator for research services begins a review of the relevant collection use, while a second review of the collection occurs to ensure that the item cannot be located. If there is reason to suspect a theft, all compiled information will be submitted to the Emory Police Department for review and investigation.

CONCLUSION

Building on what we learned in our first year with the new procedures, we currently have a plan in place to develop a back-to-basics training session with all staff members who work on the desk. In conversations with staff members, it has become apparent that there are different levels of consistency in how the reading room is handled. We plan to develop an annual refresher for both staff members and graduate student desk workers that is conducted as a workshop in order to regain and then maintain a higher level of consistency.

We are also considering reworking our reference program and implementing a researcher consultation program in which patrons will meet specifically with members of research services rather than with the person staffing the reference desk outside the reading room. While all staff members and graduate students are able to handle simple reference inquiries, involving research services to a greater degree with in-depth reference interviews will free up the desk staff to handle registration and security.

In addition, MARBL currently has a business proposal in place to implement Aeon, a special collections management system. The system would place quick, readily accessible information about patrons and collection use at the hands of whomever is working the desk, eliminating limitations in staff communications and the burden of paper record keeping. While we are just in the early stages of obtaining approval for Aeon, our hope is that we will be able to implement it in the coming year.

As previously mentioned, another large project on the horizon for MARBL is the opportunity to construct a new public space in the library for special collections. This will give us the chance to update our reading room, stacks, and reference area and allow for built-in security measures. We intend to use the opportunity provided by our new space to offer smoother policies and security that will largely go unnoticed by researchers. At present, we are trying to overcompensate for poor layout and design with an abundance of security. Careful planning for a new space will resolve many of our current concerns.

Throughout this process, one of the most useful guiding documents was the *ACRL/RBMS Guidelines Regarding Security and Theft in Special Collections*.[2] We also highly recommend participating in the Security Roundtable at SAA if you are able to attend. During the 2012 annual meeting, a NARA representative discussed recent issues in special collections and archives security and shared with the group the ways in which NARA can assist local organizations, whether or not they are part of the NARA system.[3]

Based on what we learned from the *ACRL/RBMS Guidelines*, NARA, and our own experience navigating space and technology constraints, we recommend four key steps for institutions undertaking their own security assessment:

1. Create a rubric: We were provided with one based on the *ACRL/ RBMS Guidelines* by the Emory University auditor. This document

1   **DETAILED OBSERVATIONS, RECOMMENDATIONS AND MANAGEMENT RESPONSES**

Observations	Risks and Recommendations	Management Response
1. Details	Risk Recommendations	Management Response Responsible Parties Completion Dates

Confidential – for Management and Audit and Compliance Committee use only

Figure 4.2. Sample audit template provided to MARBL by the Emory University Auditor.

(see figure 4.2) enabled us to clearly identify, categorize, and prioritize gaps and opportunities. Columns detailed ACRL/RBMS best practices, current MARBL practices and the gaps between MARBL and ACRL/RBMS, the risks posed by those gaps, and our intended response, with responsible parties and target completion date. This document also prompted discussions around what was and was not feasible.

2. Bring in outside observers to analyze and assess your procedures. Many of us are archives staff who have worked our entire professional careers in archives and special collections libraries, so our sense of what is "normal" and "expected" is therefore influenced by our professional experience and surroundings. Bringing in outside observers required us to respond to questions from those unfamiliar with archival practice; codify our needs, requirements, and limitations; and describe them for a general audience. We did this as part of our audit, but you might also consider requesting feedback from other archivists, your administration, or local law enforcement.

3. If you are the victim of a theft, share information as soon as is reasonable with institutions with similar collections or within your geographic area.

4. Maintain clearly documented policies that can be shared promptly and regularly with all staff, including permanent, part-time, and student workers as well as patrons.

No rules can eliminate the possibility that an institution will be the victim of a determined thief. But routinely, systematically, and realistically evaluating your physical space and security practices can greatly reduce the risks and show donors and patrons the care with which you maintain your collections. In striving to reach a balance between security and access, it can be difficult to update security practices in ways that do not impede ease of access or negatively affect researchers' perception of access. However, by following a clear process and establishing shared narratives for explaining security practices, we found ourselves better able to meet our patrons' needs while protecting our holdings.

Elizabeth Chase is the head of collections, assessment, and user engagement at MacPhaidin Library, Stonehill College. Until March 2013 she was the coordinator for research services at MARBL, Emory University. **Gabrielle M. Dudley** is research library fellow and **Sara Logue** is research and public services archivist at the Manuscript, Archives and Rare Book Library, Emory University.

NOTES

1. See, for example, Tricia Bishop, "Thief of Historic Documents Sentenced to Prison," *Baltimore Sun*, June 27, 2012, http://articles.baltimoresun.com/2012-06-27/news/bs-md-landau-sentenced-20120627_1_barry-h-landau-historic-documents-sentencing-date; "National Archives' Treasures Targeted by Thieves," *60 Minutes*, aired on October 28, 2012, www.cbsnews.com/8301-18560_162-57586467/national-archives-treasures-targeted-by-thieves.

2. Association of College and Research Libraries, *ACRL/RBMS Guidelines Regarding Security and Theft in Special Collections*, 2009, accessed October 11, 2013, www.ala.org/acrl/standards/security_theft.

3. Larry Evangelista and Richard Dine, "Fighting Back . . . Protecting Your Records" (presentation, Preservation Section meeting, Society of American Archivists annual meeting, Chicago, IL, August 26, 2011), www2.archivists.org/groups/preservation-section/fighting-backprotecting-your-records.

FIVE

Talking in the Night

Exploring Webchats to Serve New Audiences

Gary Brannan, West Yorkshire Archive Service

In August 2012, West Yorkshire Archive Service (WYAS) took a leap into the dark. Over the course of just two weeks, we planned and implemented a project to use a web-based chat room system ("webchat") to expand the scope of the patrons connecting with our collections. What started out as a simple experiment to promote our remote research service[1] we now feel has the potential to revolutionize remote and off-site services. Our experiences of webchats so far have expanded our ability provide reference services, opened us out to a whole new audience, and surprised us with its possibilities.

Our initial exploration of the possibilities of a webchat was driven by our recognition that we needed to contact and engage with a new, lucrative audience to stimulate demand for the research service. Like many U.K. local authority archive services, our usual on-site audience (i.e., visiting us at our service points) was reasonably easy to categorize: white, aged 45 to 74, from "prospering suburbs" or "countryside" locations,[2] and with a reasonable level of technical competence. This audience, by and large, has a demonstrable amount of leisure activity time and is willing and able to visit us during office hours. Though not strictly speaking from the local area, they have the ability to commute to our sites with relative ease.[3]

However, we knew there was an even larger potential audience for our services, that is, the audience that would happily engage with us but, for reasons of finance or geography, cannot do so. We know that for the most part this untapped audience fits roughly into a slightly younger age profile, are more technologically aware, and have less disposable leisure time.[4] Additionally, we know these potential users of our collections are part of the "boom" in interest in family history, but with limited opening hours and resources, it was difficult for us to engage with them.

Additionally, like many local services, we are in a climate of restricted budgets and falling visitor numbers. As our on-site audience declines, our remote services take on an added degree of importance, to our revenue-generating services but also in terms of our public profile. In this new age, our web services *are* our public services.

In summary, we had identified a group we really wanted to attract, but the limitations of our hours and physical location mean it was very difficult for us to engage with them using our traditional methods. We needed to find a way to do this that was quick, easy, not too demanding on staff time, and, crucially, affordable.

PLANNING

Though we are the second-largest local authority archive service in the United Kingdom, we still run on a very limited public services staffing complement, with the amount of time we were open to the public outside of normal office hours (i.e., beyond 9:30 a.m. to 5:00 p.m., Monday to Friday) restricted to just ten hours per month, with only three of these hours in the evening. These evening hours are a prime engagement time for the potential off-site user group, and it seemed a wasted opportunity to be available at a time they needed us—if only three hours a month— and not take advantage of it.

This desire to engage with a new, off-site user group tied in nicely with our need to undertake promotion for our research service. This service, for twenty-five pounds an hour, will search records in our collections on a requester's behalf. It is a revenue-generating service overseen by two professional archivists (as part of the e-services and off-site services coordinator's role and a part-time research consultant role). In 2011–2012, fees from these services resulted in just under £9,000 ($14,000). Although we needed to be mindful of the dangers of overstimulating demand, we still wanted to expand and develop this service, especially in the face of falling on-site visitor numbers.

Although we are still a busy, popular service, we know that on-site visitors have dropped by just under 50 percent over the past five years. The outlook is not all doom, however, as many of these visits have been replaced by visits to our online services, with nearly 1.25 million visits to our online genealogical resources in the last year.

Our promotional work for our services was based upon our participation earlier in the year with the BBC's successful genealogy program *Who*

Do You Think You Are?[5] In our case, we had worked with internationally renowned actor Sir Patrick Stewart. In addition to simple research work, we had been able to add further information to the structure of his family tree. In a handy addition, Jennie Kiff,[6] our research consultant, had also appeared on screen with Stewart to an estimated six million viewers as part of the program. Having this kind of publicity for our services seemed to be too good an opportunity to pass up; we wanted to build on this momentum to reach more people interested in learning about their own families' histories.

Another driving force was also a linked, long-running problem: how to transfer initial contact with inquirers into paid research work. How can we attract people to commit to paying for more in-depth research and assure them that our expertise is worth spending money on? How could we demonstrate our value, in this case for new remote audiences with whom we didn't have any personal contact? How could we convince them we were worth paying for?

This problem is part of the massive shift over the last decade or so in the way people consume family history resources. There has been an almost exponential increase in online history consumption since the launch of the 1901 census online in 2001. In the United Kingdom, this has been fueled by both Ancestry.com's and FindMyPast's further digitization efforts; a recent study showed that use of Ancestry.com grew by 20 percent in the first quarter of 2012 alone.[7] This "virtualization" of research has led to two concurrent trends: a rise in interest in archival family history resources combined with a related drop in on-site visits to archives as new users, restricted by time, location, and money, decide to undertake research at home.

We have also seen that archival research has become more of a winter activity. We know from our in-house statistics that ten to fifteen years ago the main "busy" period for our on-site services was the summer months. But there has been a definite shift toward winter activity as researchers leave their family history research while the British weather is more favorable for outdoor leisure activities. We wanted to try to find a way to let people know our services were accessible year round without needing to commit their limited free time during the peak holiday period.

To reach this group of technically savvy but time- and travel-challenged potential users, we knew we wanted to take advantage of the existing tools available to connect with them via the web. Although very early on we had already identified a live chat facility as our prime candidate, we investigated other existing alternatives already at our disposal. We have a good social media presence, particularly on Twitter. As of April 2013, we have nearly three thousand followers on Twitter, with a smaller footprint on Facebook of nearly two hundred fans. We have a very active following on Twitter, and it would have been possible to use this for some kind of live inquiry service. In fact, we already do; "social media" is now a standard category on our inquiries database.

However, the 140-character limitation would have proved impossible to work with. We needed something where we could (within reason) type to our heart's content. Facebook would have solved that problem, but for the most part, it is still a growing outlet for us, used as a supplementary communications channel and photo-display area. Facebook is for us still a tool in search of a need. We have a presence there, and we try to keep it active, but it doesn't generate the kind of engagement from active users that we were looking for. Both Facebook and Twitter, even if used in a messaging capacity, were restricted either by their need for membership or their technical limitations (such as Twitter's character limit).

Going through this exercise and considering what options wouldn't work helped us come up with a list of our ideal specifications for the tool we needed to communicate with our untapped remote audience:

- The system needed to be dynamic, with a "back and forth" question-and-answer routine.
- We wanted to include links to other websites (such as our records on www.ancestry.co.uk or our mental health collections on www.historytoherstory.org.uk).
- Conversations needed to take place in a space where everyone could join in if they wanted to, with no need or option for a private chat facility.
- The system needed to allow for moderation of user comments.
- It needed to be able to run on the smallest amount of staff available.
- We needed something that would work with minimal IT support.
- The tool needed to allow customizable user names so that we could identify ourselves and users could define their own online identities.

We had another primary requirement: cost. The system needed to be free and require minimal time investment. Taking all this into account, our first choice, webchat, seemed the ideal solution if we could find the right tool to implement.

Additionally, as with any online project, it was crucial that we obtained firm management support for the experiment. As this idea came via one of our research service planning meetings (which include our public services and access manager), this was not a problem in our case. WYAS has a good culture of experimentation; if you have a good idea and it sounds workable, you are encouraged to develop it further. In our case, we knew our ideas were feasible in a technical sense, and we thankfully had a good previous track record of developing workable ideas.[8]

Last, but certainly by no means least, we had to get our IT department on board. This was reasonably easy, though they obviously had their concerns about how it would all work out. However, they entered into the project with enthusiasm and ended up giving us all the support we needed. Several systems were considered before James Waugh[9] in our IT department suggested AJAX Chat, a system that seemed to meet all our requirements. AJAX Chat is a free and fully customizable webchat system and so does not require users to have any preinstalled software (although it does require some installation for the webchat host). It's really almost a "walk up and go" piece of software from the user's point of view, which is one of the things we really wanted from a system. Crucially, in addition to the technical considerations, AJAX Chat also gave us the following key requirements:

- the ability to eject and ban offending users,
- a visible list of current online users with a user menu (this was vital if we were to keep a log of how many users we actually had),
- emoticons/smilies—we wanted it to be friendly,
- embedded clickable hyperlinks,
- splitting of long words to preserve chat layout,
- ability to delete messages inside the chat,
- ability to define opening hours for the chat,
- support for multiple languages (especially useful if we needed to quote in another language, specifically Latin in our case),
- ability to enter line breaks (we'd need in some cases to preserve paragraph breaks, and we decided early on that we'd try and keep the responses coherent), and
- ability to work with all modern browsers, especially in Firefox and Internet Explorer.[10]

Actual installation and customization of the system was a reasonably quick process—just over a few days from selecting the software to testing the system (although in the end we ran quite close to our deadline). Some of the features we'd identified as desirable ended up being superfluous in our first live session, but it's important to remember that we wanted to develop a system for the long term, so we wanted to include features we didn't especially need at that point in time. In terms of actual development time, it took James about half a day to find AJAX Chat, with about one and a half days needed to get it installed and working and an additional day to brand and modify it with our custom settings. After this initial work, the actual setup and closedown time for IT for each webchat session was just twenty minutes.

Staff training was thankfully minimal in scope, as the built-in moderator interface was reasonably self-explanatory. IT was able to give us a test chat log-in, so we were able to use the chat over the course of a day or so to get used to it. We felt that although we didn't need to be experts (especially in our first few sessions), we did, at least, need to be competent. One of the major benefits of AJAX Chat was that it was entirely free (barring staff time in terms of development and running the system), so we were in the position that any research service work that was commissioned over these sessions would effectively more than pay for itself. Any income we generated would be all profit (again, aside from the investment of staff time). However, it is worth noting that although the system is free, there may be extra costs in terms of structural IT systems if that is needed.

With our tool selected, we now needed to decide when to host our first webchat session. We knew we needed to make sure we ran the events at a time when our desired user group would be available. We'd been considering our options for some months, but once we settled on using webchat to reach new users, everything fell into place quite quickly. We knew we wanted to run our first session during one of the monthly evening periods when our physical research rooms are open so that none of us would have to work extra evening hours. As we were considering when to launch our effort, it just so happened that Jennie Kiff, our research consultant, and I (e-services coordinator but a trained public services archivist) were scheduled to work the next late Monday session at our Wakefield office. Timing was important; we didn't want to clash with any competing events, such as *Who Do You Think You Are?*, which was broadcast on Thursday evenings at the time. While running a webchat session during a time when we were also responsible for serving in-person researchers meant possibly balancing the needs of both a busy webchat and a busy reading room, we needed to make sure we weren't placing any unnecessary burdens upon both our staff (in terms of time) and the resources of the service (financially) by working beyond normal hours.

Taking this into consideration, our pilot chat was penciled in for August 24, 2012, 6:00 to 8:00 p.m., to be staffed by Jennie and me during our regular evening shift. Our IT contact also needed to be online to open and close the chat room and make the link live via our main website, but he was able to do this remotely and didn't mind logging in during the evening hours to help out.

With the software selected and installed and the time and place set for our first session, Jennie and I considered what else we would need. We knew we'd need to have various resource materials on hand to help us, specifically our electronic catalog and reference works. An added bonus was that, for our pilot chat, we were in the same building as some of our collections, so for some questions, we knew we might be able to actually find the information a user was requesting from the records immediately, too. These considerations really demonstrated that we needed to be in the office to do this. While technically we could probably have run the chats from the comfort of our own homes, the results would not have been as productive.

One other form of support we employed, though not strictly speaking needed, was that other on-duty staff from other locations were asked to populate the webchat room as well as Jennie and me. This was done in part to make the room appear full, as often new users will feel reluctant to stay or participate in an empty room. Therefore it was helpful to have a few users already waiting in the room to pad it out a bit, encourage contribution, and help wherever necessary.

In our case, we didn't ask our colleagues to identify themselves as also being staff of the archives. We wanted our users to feel more comfortable from having a prepopulated room, but we didn't want them to feel that they were outnumbered by the professionals! There are, of course, some ethical issues to take into account with this approach, but we felt this was a calculated risk that, in the end, paid off. However, this will all depend on your own staff and how you feel about such practices. For us, especially in our first trial, having a more crowded room with some familiar "faces" made us feel more confident.

In our case, Alison, one of our archive assistants at Wakefield, ended up helping us out with some questions, which was greatly appreciated because we ended up being busier than we expected. As a case of best practice, once Alison began helping, we asked her to change her user name to make it clear that she was actually archive staff.

IMPLEMENTATION

We opened the doors to the webchat at 6:00 p.m. on August 24, 2012, with no real sense of how it might work or even if it would work at all. Would the system be accessible? Would the users be able to navigate the tricky first log-in page (something we were desperate to replace or simplify)? Would the system crash? And—and this played on my mind most of all—would anyone actually want to use it in the first place? We had given the webchat plenty of promotion online via Twitter, but we knew that all the promotion in the world couldn't help an unpopular idea.

From this point on, we were on a blank page. We'd no real preconceptions about how the sessions would go. As new users entered the session, Jennie or I would introduce ourselves to them, ask if they had a question, and then try and help them on a one-to-one basis. This seemed to coax many of the reluctant users out of their shells and make them much more willing to talk to us, as they were able to develop a personal relationship with us. And of course, everyone else in the room could watch these one-on-one interactions. Our user names made it clear that the user was talking to a member of archive staff because we had the suffix *archive* to our user names (e.g., gary_archive).

We were pleasantly surprised to see the numbers in the room go up slowly and steadily. As the evening wore on, it was a case of typing as quickly and coherently as we could; we were welcoming new users, answering inquiries already on the go, and trying to keep chat going at the same time (see figure 5.1).

It was during this period that we found that we could barely keep up with the number of users in the room, and we were starting to feel the effect of underestimating how popular the webchat would be. As it stood, we were at the limit of our capability, and we were able to keep up (even if the reality was that at times it very nearly fell off the rails). Had we had just another five concurrent users, things could have been very different indeed, and what was in the end a positive thing could easily have been a publicity nightmare as we failed to keep up with demand. We were lucky that numbers in the physical reading room had dropped off reasonably early, so we were able to devote our time solely to the webchat as it hit its peak. We rode out luck, and it paid off, but it could easily have gone the other way, so we were very lucky that we had "extra" staff on hand to help.

As the night drew on, more and more users entered the room, including our first (self-proclaimed) visitor from North America (Canada, to be precise). We were really struggling to keep up with each other, as we were based in two separate rooms, so we actually reconvened to a spare

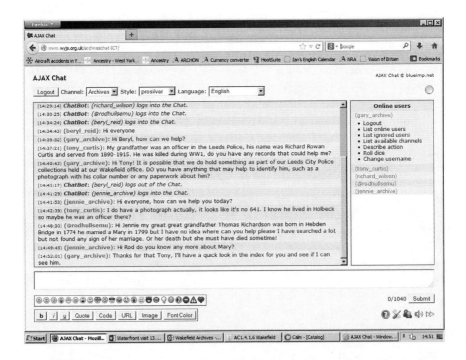

Figure 5.1.   The webchat interface, illustrating the challenges of multi-user chat.

office so we could be closer to each other and could better communicate between us who was handling which user and give each other occasional advice about answering questions. (In retrospect this is another reason we couldn't have supported the chat session from the comfort of our own sofas!)

We closed the chat room at 8:00 p.m., with several users joining us in the last half hour or so—testament to the fact that we could have run the event for much longer than we originally anticipated.

RESULTS

For those of us involved, the end of the pilot chat came as a massive relief. The system had worked. We had attracted users, managed to be diverting while juggling more activity than we were prepared for, and the session had been useful for all those involved. Crucially, we had also managed to stimulate some research service income. Our management team was very supportive and saw the potential in the project. Our head of service made time to pop into the chat room in the first webchat to see how things were going and expressed her positive thoughts afterward, which was a real boost.

We scheduled our next webchat session for the same hours on Monday, October 29. We used the mold of the first pilot chat as far as process and didn't make any major changes at all, as we felt everything had worked effectively. While we felt the second chat went well, we were concerned that we didn't get as many users as we had for the first session. However, we soon realized that our session was coinciding with extreme weather on America's east coast in the form of Hurricane Sandy.

However, we didn't think we could blame everything on the weather, so we decided to move the next webchat's time to the U.K. lunch break. We held the third session on Monday, February 8, 2013. This chat went extremely well—twenty-one users in all—with us having two extra staff from our Leeds and Bradford offices involved to field questions from their districts.

We were wary about the possible fallout from the second webchat; the drop in numbers would need explaining if we were to convince others the project was worthwhile taking forward. The second webchat had had more publicity, but the best explanation was that many of our potential U.S.-based chatters would have been affected by Hurricane Sandy and therefore, rightly, had other issues on their mind. The third chat showed how the numbers could stay reasonably static overall and gave us the boost to continue them. The statistics for the three sessions were:

- August 24, 2012, 6:00 p.m. to 8:00 p.m.: twenty-seven attendees
- October 29, 2012, 6:00 p.m. to 8:00 p.m.: ten attendees
- February 8, 2013, 12:00 p.m. to 2:00 p.m.: twenty-one attendees

While the numbers varied, our users were very impressed with the system and chats we undertook. The feedback we received was exceptionally positive. These comments via our users on Twitter (i.e., the user group we were aiming for) are typical of the response:

- Thank you—it was fun and very interesting.
- Gr8 vibe MT @wyorksarchives Our fingers r aflame w/ ideas! We might just have found a relation 2 the Brontes! . . . free #familyhistory
- @wyorksarchives didn't get chance to chat v. much as joined in late and was using phone . . . so slow! Ah well, have emailed as suggested.
- Ok challenge those experts everyone RT @wyorksarchives: One hour to go until FREE webchat with our research experts bit.ly/VKZc2U
- Clever approach
- Thanks to Jenni [*sic*] & Gary @wyorksarchives for their help this evening. Appreciated :)

One interesting discovery is that we didn't see any return visitors to the chats, which either suggests we put people off from returning or that we managed to help most in their initial chat. We're inclined to believe it was the latter. We didn't witness anyone who seemed uncomfortable or discouraged by their experience with us. Most of the problems we were faced with were more along the lines of what we'd call a "difficult" beginner inquiry, such as a search for a missing relative in the recent past (usually in a prison or hospitals context), details of a local business, or more complex and involved inquiries involving "missing links" in an already developed family tree. The response of the users indicated they were all very much in favor of us doing more. Ironically, the group who wanted them to run again the most were the ones who had missed the original sessions and wanted to join in later. Beyond that, we could also look at the reactions of our staff and management, all of whom seemed to be happy with the way things had gone.

While we had a sense that users had enjoyed their experiences, we wanted to provide some sort of more formal evaluation. We hadn't considered this aspect earlier, as we didn't even know if the project itself would work. Our main barometer of success was, of course, user numbers. Not only was this measurable, but also this was effectively a show of support from the very people we were seeking to contact. Pleasingly, numbers grew over the period of the webchats, with the exception of the session we believe was affected by Hurricane Sandy, which showed that more and more users were joining in as the sessions went along.

However, we were certainly also interested in using the number of research service requests generated as a form of assessment. So far we've generated just over one hundred pounds in income. This, while not a stellar figure by any means, still represents excellent value on the return for the experiment, considering all but staff time was free of charge and the general value of the chat sessions in promoting our services overall. We hope some people who attended the chat sessions may return to us later when they are ready for more detailed research.

We know that we'd like to hold more chats and to make it a full part of our user experience. We have established that there is an audience out there who would like to interact with us and are more than happy to contribute. We've started to develop further topics and ideas of where to take the chats beyond just an open call to submit questions. We'd like to move toward themed or targeted chats based around specific topics (such as criminal or school records) to give the rather disparate chats a bit more focus. We would also like to make them much more regular, for instance, once a month at a set time, to create and build a regular audience. We may also consider moving chats to suit a particular time zone outside the United Kingdom, such as the United States, or, more ambitiously, Australia and New Zealand.

Beyond this, we'd like to extend the chat room concept further to include audio and video. Development of our website continues, too, and we think there are definite possibilities in terms of embedding the chat facility permanently within it as a virtual meeting space. In terms of "real estate" it's great; running costs are low, occupancy is high, staffing needs are small, and opening hours are virtually unlimited!

LESSONS LEARNED

In terms of the lessons we've learned, we can't stress enough the need to get management approval. Although we did not see this in our experience, we were very much aware that a webchat does not come without risks. Spam users, pornbots, potential libel issues, and flame wars are all very real risks when you invite the entire Internet to your door. As I mentioned, in our first session, we were concerned at many points that we wouldn't be able to keep up with the demand and the whole thing would make us look like we didn't know what we were doing. While there are no great technical problems in implementing the system and the software is freely available, as we found out, there are definite risks in terms of reputational damage from something going awry.

We assessed these risks and took various steps to mitigate them, but they do exist, and you need to be honest with your management team as to what could go wrong and demonstrate that you are taking the necessary steps to avoid a catastrophe. In our case we were surprised at how speedily we were able to convince our managers, but in more risk-averse climates, this process could take some time.

In retrospect, the greatest lesson we learned would be to get IT on board, keep them on board, and let them lead the technical development of the system. We took the right approach by clearly identifying what we wanted (and didn't want); then we let them pick a system that best met those needs and that they knew they could support. The involvement of a committed IT professional is crucial. Many of the best systems require a level of technological skill beyond that of the average archivist. This is where patience is also key. It may take some time for you to convince others that a chat system, which may certainly be viewed with some suspicion, is really something they want to try to support. In our case we were able to make a clear case that the tool fitted an immediate need.

One unexpected, and somewhat amusing in hindsight, lesson came from the disparity between today's meanings for words and their use in historic terminology. One of our additional requirements was the need for the system to have a good profanity filter, as we were concerned about the impact of spammers/mischievous users. With this in mind, we chose a system with a good, preinstalled filter system. However, we soon ran into trouble, as we found that some common record categories were being masked automatically. This caused most problems with such words as *bastardy* (which was presented as *b******y*). This was not only confusing for an inexperienced customer, but it also looked like we were being unnecessarily squeamish. Thankfully, during testing I had a fun half hour trying all sorts of potentially blocked terms that we needed and had them removed from the filter! In this case, the solution ended up being an easy one, but it's a good example of how seemingly innocuous issues, easily overlooked, can potentially cause problems, even with the most well-meaning reasoning.

Another unanticipated problem—although in some respects a happy one—was that we underestimated how popular our offering would be. We initially set our sights low. We should, in hindsight, have been prepared for success rather than worry about failure. When the room filled up, both Jennie and I were at the limits of what we could cope with, and we wished we had drafted in more staff (which we did on subsequent occasions). If you happen to attract a bigger crowd, be prepared for sore fingers.

Finally, we also now know that we can extend these tools further with our research service, using the chat room as an organized meeting space for individual or smaller group "appointments." In this model users could meet with our research consultant on a one-to-one basis for a longer live chat, much the same as having an appointment with Jennie in the office but at a time and place much more convenient to the user. At the moment we don't offer face-to-face consultation, but this kind of virtual consultation space could be a potential new income stream in the future.

We have no doubt whatsoever that there is a very bright and promising future for our webchat system; it's just a case of finding the right format and applying it in the right way. The possibilities are very exciting and, indeed, intriguing; the idea of a virtual meeting space, already developed, and free of charge is very attractive, especially in our context of a multisite service.

CONCLUSION

The webchats open us up to a new, lucrative, engageable audience. They provide customers with immediate access to professional support and knowledge in a much less formal (and bureaucratic) environment. The chats made us seem more approachable and human, and we were able to place ourselves in times and places where our users were and not the other way around. We became a seamless, ubiquitous, accessible archive service.

However, this is not to say that we found a flawless medium. We now know that, in terms of in-depth research, the chats can only ever be superficial. Large numbers of users meant we were in danger of losing an inquiry, and the amount of concentrated time meant that it would be difficult for a member of staff to undertake other duties (such as reading room supervision) and take part in a webchat. We certainly underestimated the amount of concentration and mental agility needed, as we were working on our toes for the full duration. To engage users in other time zones, you may also have to be prepared to work well beyond normal—and sociable—hours.

There are also other, deeper issues. The instant nature of a webchat means that, often, inquirers may expect an instant, full, and correct answer, something that's not always possible. Beyond this we are, by definition, restricting ourselves to just the web literate. Is this the right thing to do? As in our case we were actively seeking to meet and engage with this group, we were absolutely fine with this, but it's something to bear in mind when planning a webchat: Does your organization have concerns about providing enhanced access to reference services for only those able to use the webchat, too?

For us the webchats have proved to be a powerful, near limitless tool, allowing us to open ourselves wider to new audiences, to be accessible in different places than we could even be in terms of a physical location. In effect, by using webchats, we've opened a new office, a new space in which to meet our users. Don't think of it as a chat room; think of it as a virtual research room. And so, although we may be located in West Yorkshire, now we know that the world is at our door. It is up to us to welcome them.[11]

Gary Brannan is the e-services and off-site services coordinator, West Yorkshire Archive Service.

NOTES

My thanks go to Jennie Kiff and James Waugh for their help in compiling this case study.

1. The research service still exists but was rebranded as "Ask the Experts" in April 2013. This was further subdivided into short, standard, and express services. The webchat referred to here was built for the "standard" service.

2. Archives and Records Association Public Services and Quality Group (PSQG), *Survey of Visitors to U.K. Archives 2011*, 2011, accessed March 30, 2013, www.archives.org.uk/images/documents/National_Report_2011.pdf.

3. Ibid.

4. See Archives and Records Association (UK and Ireland), Public Services Quality Group (PSQG), *Distance User Survey 2013*, 2013..

5. Since 2005 this television series has helped U.K. celebrities trace their family trees. With viewing figures of nearly six million, it is one of the most powerful drivers in U.K. amateur genealogy.

6. Jennie Kiff is archive assistant and research consultant. Jennie oversees the work of our "Ask the Experts" service for two days per week (fourteen hours full-time equivalent).

7. More statistics related to the growth of online genealogy providers can be found at "Top Trends in Genealogy," *Genealogy in Time Magazine*, June 2012, accessed May 3, 2013, http://www.genealogyintime.com/GenealogyResources/Articles/top%20trends% 20in%20genealogy%20page%2001.html.

8. For instance, the World War II bombing Twitter project conducted via the West Riding ARP Twitter account (www.twitter.com/WR_ARP).

9. James Waugh, WYJS, works as part of our corporate IT department and led development of the technical side of the webchats.

10. "AJAX Chat," *AJAX Chat*, accessed April 30, 2013, http://frug.github.io/AJAX-Chat.

11. For more information, contact Gary Brannan via gbrannan@wyjs.org.uk or on Twitter as @gbrannanarchive.

SIX

A Small Shop Meets a Big Challenge

*Finding Creative Ways to Assist the Researchers of the
Breath of Life Archival Institute for Indigenous
Languages*

Leanda Gahegan and Gina Rappaport, National Anthropological Archives, Smithsonian Institution

In 2011, the Smithsonian Institution's National Anthropological Archives (NAA) hosted one of the largest group research visits in its 184-year history—the first Breath of Life (BOL) Archival Institute for Indigenous Languages. The goal of BOL is to teach native-language learners how to utilize archival resources to resurrect endangered languages. For two weeks, sixty researchers visited the NAA and worked with a number of archival collections. This visit posed an unprecedented challenge to our archives' staff of five, and we responded by developing creative solutions to problems of staffing, reading room space, and collection access.

In spite of the challenges, we knew we had to strategize expanding our space, access to collections, and staffing numbers to successfully host this program. This opportunity was mutually beneficial to the BOL participants and the NAA. It gave us an opportunity to facilitate access to our collections, support the revitalization of native languages, and introduce a diverse group of researchers to our archives. Our rich resources and experience with language revitalization projects made the NAA an ideal repository to host the first national Breath of Life Institute.

The NAA is the nation's main repository for original documentation for spoken, endangered, and extinct Native American languages. Approximately 250 languages are represented in the collection, and for many of these, documentation is found nowhere else in the world. The origin of the NAA dates back to the founding of the Bureau of American Ethnology (BAE) in 1879 by John Wesley Powell, who was one of the leaders of the early federal geological surveys of the American west. Through his many encounters with Native American communities, Powell became aware that the traditional knowledge, language, and life ways were being constantly threatened by western encroachment. In response, Powell founded the BAE and developed a staff of anthropologists to conduct research in Native North American communities, documenting language and culture. Powell also consolidated the ethnographic records created and collected during the early surveys—primarily those led by Ferdinand Hayden, George Wheeler, and Powell himself. In addition, the BAE absorbed linguistic and other ethnological records and data collected by the Smithsonian since the 1850s. Over the course of eighty-six years, the BAE archives grew with the field research of its staff and material collected through collaborative work and donations. In 1965, the archives of the BAE and the Smithsonian Museum of Natural History Department of Anthropology's archives merged. In 1968, these combined archives were renamed the National Anthropological Archives.

In addition to indigenous North American language material, the NAA has significant collections relating to Mesoamerican, Australian, and other indigenous languages from throughout the world. The NAA's collections comprise more than 12,000 cubic feet of archival material containing roughly 7,000 individual manuscripts, collections of personal papers and organizational records, more than a million photographs, 10,000 works of art, and thousands of sound recordings. NAA's holdings are heavily consulted by communities seeking documentation on their languages and cultural heritages, and linguistic documentation in the collections includes vocabularies, grammars, lexicons, sound recordings, and other material.

Organizationally, the NAA is part of the Department of Anthropology in the Smithsonian Institution's National Museum of Natural History (NMNH). Physically, it is located in the Museum Support Center (MSC), the collections and research facility for NMNH located nine miles outside of Washington, DC, in Suitland, MD. The MSC houses the collections for NMNH in five state-of-the-art storage spaces, dubbed "pods"; each pod is approximately the size of a football field and can contain everything from archival papers to several giant squid specimens in ethanol. MSC also houses workspace and laboratories for various NMNH departments besides anthropology, including botany, paleobiology, mineral sciences, and entomology.

PLANNING

The Breath of Life Archival Institute for Indigenous Languages is based on a one-week workshop model developed by the Advocates for Indigenous California Language Survival (AICLS) in partnership with the University of California at Berkeley in the early 1990s. This biennial workshop brings together indigenous Californians, who are working toward language revitalization in their communities, with linguists to mine endangered language resources held in archives. With instruction in linguistics and research methods coupled with research in archives, the workshop is a powerful educational event that supports linguistic and cultural revival within California tribes. The success of the California BOL workshop inspired the national BOL in Washington, DC, which opened this educational and research opportunity to tribes across the nation. The national BOL project was funded by the Documenting Endangered Languages program of the National Science Foundation and the National Endowment for the Humanities with sponsorship from the Endangered Language Fund.

The NAA has supported a variety of language and traditional knowledge revitalization efforts and is an active part of the language revitalization community. Microfilm copies of one of our prominent collections, the John Peabody Harrington papers, were heavily used in the California BOL workshops. Prior to writing their grant, the organizers of the California workshops contacted our former director, Dr. Robert Leopold, about the possibility of a national BOL program held at the NAA to utilize our expansive collections of language documentation. Dr. Leopold agreed to host the program.

Because the NAA was an early supporter of BOL, we were already familiar with the organizers. Our involvement in the early planning stages of BOL was crucial to the success of this project. We needed to speak openly to the organizers about limitations regarding collection access, staffing, and space. It was important for us to manage the expectations of the organizers and clarify what was and was not possible. We communicated that we needed additional funds for duplication and staffing to host this program. Therefore, they were able to write some of these funds into the grant proposal.

Once funding for BOL was approved, we initiated planning for the institute to visit the NAA. We began the work of devising logistical and practical procedures for BOL approximately seven months before the June start date. During this preparation stage, Leanda Gahegan, reference archivist, spent more than two hundred hours planning, scheduling, training staff, and meeting with BOL organizers. Other archival staff devoted time toward the selection and digitization of material. Planning to meet the needs of these visitors was a major focus of all our activities in early 2011.

One of the first steps in our planning process was to identify significant language source material in our collections. We had a general estimate of the language groups represented in our collections but performed a number of keyword searches in our online catalog system to refine our list. We were very fortunate that we had already dedicated prior time and staff resources toward an enhanced cataloging project for our language collection. This project involved a large amount of research into different spellings of language groups, tribal groups, and regions. For instance, the collection titled "MS 4121: Comparative Vocabularies of Southeastern and Gulf Languages 1916–1917" contains material related to more than twenty-one tribal groups and languages. We included all the appropriate subject headings in this catalog record to make these kinds of general language collections discoverable to researchers.

We also added the subject heading "Language and Languages—Documentation" to all appropriate catalog records. This subject heading allowed us to quickly identify relevant language collections. A simple search for this subject heading retrieves 5,525 catalog records. We should note that some of our collections of photographs and manuscripts are cataloged at the item level. While it's true that, from a traditional archival point of view, item-level cataloging should be avoided, these records proved to be extremely useful to increase collection discoverability and best meet the needs of our primary users.

After our research we created a comprehensive list of languages represented in our collections, organized by significance, relevancy, and quantity. This list was very helpful to the BOL organizers, who used it to narrow down participant applications. The organizers carefully selected only those participants who were studying languages with available archival source material at the NAA. Once participants were accepted, we could start to identify collections of interest for BOL groups and brainstorm how to provide access to this material. Participants were divided into groups of language learners and linguists; the size of the groups ranged from three to five people each.

Collection access was our biggest challenge. Much of the original source material contains information related to a number of different languages, and as such, different researchers would potentially be interested in the same source material at the same time. Because the Breath of Life Institute was pairing individuals to perform collaborative research, we realized that the archive needed to provide "workable" copies of collection material for all participants. Preferably, these copies needed to be in paper form, able to be passed between partners and marked upon.

At first, we considered just providing black-and-white photocopies of material to the participants, but after speaking to previous linguistics researchers, we realized that these wouldn't be suitable. Many linguistic texts have interlinear translations or other notations written in various shades of ink that would be lost in black-and-white copies. We also considered providing our existing microform copies of material to patrons, but this also had the problems of faded or unreadable text, and we only had two microform readers. Therefore, we knew we needed to provide researchers with either original source material or a color surrogate. Color photocopies were cost prohibitive, so we chose to create digital surrogates. We combined the funding from BOL with grant funds from our Save America's Treasures (SAT) grant to digitize some of our language collections.

In 2010, the NAA received a $323,000 grant from the SAT program to conduct a condition survey of its early manuscript collection, hire a paper conservator to stabilize selected material, and digitize thousands of pages. We combined funds from this SAT grant with funds from BOL to digitize, rehouse, and perform minor conservation treatments on linguistic documents vital for BOL research. These documents included bound vocabularies, large maps, photographs, small notebooks, and other paper-based archival material dated from the 1860s through the 1940s in varying states of degradation. Many items needed preservation work before scanning. Luckily, the goals of the SAT grant and BOL research were mutually compatible.

Approximately six months in advance of BOL, we worked with the curator of linguistics for the Smithsonian's NMNH and others to select material for digitization. Selection was based on usefulness and importance to the approximately twenty-four languages under study. This process was lengthy and involved a high level of coordination and communication between the curator, our digitization manager, BOL organizers, and other archives staff. We created a detailed Microsoft Excel spreadsheet tracking items that the BOL organizers identified as important, the curator analyzed, and our digitization manager approved for scanning. During this planning process, we identified and digitized at least one significant archival manuscript for each language group represented in BOL. Because BOL supported funding for digitization, we were able to distribute the digital surrogates to participants at no charge.

Once material was digitized, we either placed it online through our catalog or loaded the files onto the one public computer in the reading room. We also created a personalized flash drive for each BOL participant with relevant finding aids, digital surrogates of language material, maps of the BOL meeting areas, schedules, and other documents. Not all of the participants had laptops, but at least one member of each language group research team had a laptop on which to view the files. The flash drive delivery was well received and solved our challenge of multiple researchers needing to see the same material. Participants could take turns with the original documents but still use them electronically.

Our second challenge was our small staff size. We needed more staff to accommodate sixty BOL researchers. The NAA has a staff of approximately five full-time positions, with only one reference archivist dedicated to scheduling and handling on-site visits. Normally, the largest number of researchers we can accommodate at one time is ten individuals. At first, we simply couldn't imagine how we could accommodate sixty researchers at once. We brainstormed a number of possible staffing scenarios, including limiting the number of researchers per day, hiring additional staff, recruiting volunteers and interns, and "borrowing" staff from within the archives for reference duties. Due to the time constraints of the BOL schedule and high research demand, we were unable to limit the number of researchers per day. We also couldn't hire additional staff because of budget restrictions. Therefore our best option was to recruit volunteers and interns and request that all available NAA staff help with reference duties during BOL.

Our efforts to increase our staff yet still maintain a high standard of service involved an intern recruitment campaign started in late February 2011. We focused on graduate-level students enrolled in archival programs and advertised through archival e-mail distribution lists. The deadline for applications was late March, and the internship started in May. We wanted to offer stipends for the interns, but NAA's meager operating budget couldn't support it. Fortunately, we were able to secure funding for one intern from the Summer Institute in Museum Anthropology (SIMA) that was scheduled to take place at the NAA immediately following BOL. We calculated that we needed at least two interns for this project and negotiated with the BOL organizers to secure funding for a second intern position. Coincidentally, during the intern selection process, we were approached by a suitable undergraduate student in linguistics from the University of Alberta, Canada, who was available to come intern during BOL, fully funded by her university.

These three carefully selected and fully funded interns formed the core of our BOL reference team. The team was expanded to include current volunteers, interns, and available NAA staff. Once the team was established, we planned a number of orientation and training sessions. During these sessions, we reviewed reading room procedures so that everyone was comfortable working with researchers and explaining research policies.

We also emphasized and relied upon the *Protocols for Native American Archival Materials* (www2.nau.edu/libnap-p) for best practices and guidelines. The *Protocols* were extremely useful as a tool to introduce some of the challenges and complexities inherent in working with cultural property source material. The majority of the holdings of the NAA document indigenous cultures, and the information contained within these collections can be sensitive, sacred, private, or proprietary. Often we do not know how sensitive, sacred, or private until these issues are brought to our attention by members of the source community.

The *Protocols for Native American Archival Materials* section on accessibility and use was invaluable to us while we were training our interns.

We emulated the guidelines for action, especially the directive to create welcoming communities of research in reading rooms, and consulted the glossary of terms often. Because some of our interns were unfamiliar with the nature of Native American archival material, they found the section on culturally sensitive material especially helpful. Some of our language material contains information that could be defined as specialized or sacred knowledge. The *Protocols* include a useful list of examples of archival material that may contain culturally sensitive information. We consulted this list and made sure to handle this material carefully and with much respect.

Space for accommodating all sixty BOL researchers at the NAA was another immediate and pressing concern. Our reading room has only three tables and ten chairs. We knew immediately that we needed to secure additional space for research. Our most viable option was to establish satellite reading rooms within our building, the MSC. This would allow us to increase our space for researchers and still maintain a high degree of control over the reference interactions. We booked two additional spaces as satellite reading rooms for the two weeks of BOL. These spaces were a building library and a conference room. The small, on-site library had plenty of tables and was not heavily used by building staff, making it a perfect space for a temporary reading room that could accommodate thirty people. The conference room was a narrow space with one long table that could accommodate approximately fifteen people. Even with these additional spaces, we didn't have quite as much space as we would have liked, but it was the best we could do while keeping all the researchers on site and therefore close to the collections. We planned for the NAA reading room to become extra cozy and seat a few more people than it normally would, and we crossed our fingers that we would be able to work around any problems.

IMPLEMENTATION

The Breath of Life Archival Institute for Endangered Languages began on June 13, 2011. During the two weeks of BOL, participants had a full schedule of lectures, research visits, instruction, homework, and presentations. A typical day started at 8:30 a.m. with breakfast and announcements, two and a half hours of instruction, lunch, and then approximately four hours spent in an archival repository, possibly the NAA. The instructions ranged in subject from how to utilize archival materials in language revitalization projects and introduction to grammar and phonetics to basics of archival research and intellectual property and how to create useful lesson plans for language curriculum.

The BOL organizers divided participants into four groups based on language families or tribal groups. For example, all participants from

California Indian tribes were in group 1, while participants from south-eastern Indian tribes were in group 2. During the first four days of BOL (Monday to Thursday), these groups met with BOL faculty for workshops and lessons in the mornings and had orientations and tours in the afternoon. While one group was at the NAA's reading room for their orientation, the other groups were either on a tour with collections staff of the Smithsonian's NMNH Department of Anthropology, at an orientation with staff of the Library of Congress American Folklife Center, or with the staff of the archives of the Smithsonian's National Museum of the American Indian.

For the NAA orientation, staff presented an overview of the archives' history and holdings, reviewed reading room policies, explained MSC security guidelines, and distributed the participant flash drives. We also set up a small show-and-tell with photographs or manuscript material from the archives that were relevant to the communities of the tour groups. Following the orientation, all staff worked with participants for several hours to identify collections of interest in our online catalog and plan for the following week's research (see figure 6.1). During these orientations we also presented groups with a list of suggested collections of interest. These lists were generated during our research stage in the planning process. While it was repetitive for staff to give the same presentation for four straight days, we felt it was easier to work with the smaller groups and provide individualized instruction on our catalog and archival policies.

After the orientation sessions, participants submitted collections requests to the BOL organizers, who completed individual call slips for collection material and created a pull list spreadsheet for NAA staff. On Friday, we used this spreadsheet to create reading room assignments based on research teams and language groups. Often different research teams requested the same manuscript material, so we tried to assign these teams to the same room. We chose to keep participants in the same room for the duration of BOL. For example, the Penobscot research team was assigned to the library reading room for all of their research visits. This made it easier for staff and research teams.

The BOL participants were scheduled for archival research in the afternoons of Monday through Thursday of their second week. Because participants could visit a number of archives, we weren't sure of the total number of individuals visiting the NAA on any particular day. Each morning, participants signed up with a BOL representative to visit the NAA. The representative would then e-mail us the sign-up sheet so we had a general idea of the number of participants for that day. However, we understood that this number was only an estimate and prepared to accommodate all participants at one time. We also created flexibility in the event of last-minute changes in researcher schedules. For instance, when one research team canceled an appointment at another archive to

Figure 6.1.   Breath of Life participants in the NAA reading room. Intern Whitney Hopkins (standing back, left) and Curator of Linguistics Gabriela Pèrez Bàez (standing front, left) are assisting researchers in using the online catalog to locate relevant records. *Photo by Stephanie Christensen*

spend more time at the NAA, we were able to make room for them and retrieve their materials quickly.

Because researchers were arriving in the afternoon, we pulled collections in the morning and placed the material in the assigned reading room location. During BOL we used a small army of collection carts to pull material for participants. In the mornings we had a train of seventeen carts traveling between our storage space and the reading rooms. We organized collections and carts by research team and assigned reading room location. In order to keep track of collections, we attached a list of cart contents, research team information, and reading room location to the cart. At the end of the day, we cross-referenced this list against the contents of the cart and noted the collections to be reshelved. Depending on the sign-up information from the BOL representative that we received each morning, we pulled new collections and generated an updated list for each cart. One intern was responsible for the creation and managements of these lists.

Once BOL researchers arrived at the NAA, carts loaded with their prerequested material were in their assigned reading rooms. We pre-equipped all satellite reading rooms with such supplies as pencils, digital camera use and photocopy order forms, gloves, place markers, book cradles, and paper weights. Researchers were encouraged to use digital cameras to take pictures of manuscripts and photographs. If researchers wanted photocopies of material, they needed to place an official copy order. We offered a small discount on our regular photocopying prices. Because a number of these photocopy orders were large, we notified researchers that it would take a couple of months to process. We also provided copies of our permission request form.

We also assigned NAA staff members and interns (one staff member and one intern) to a reading room. Research teams were also assigned to the same room for the entire week to allow them to become comfortable with their surroundings, settle in, and develop a rapport with the NAA staff assisting them. At the same time, NAA staff got to know the researchers in their locations and provided individualized support. We also had several staff roaming between rooms or on call; this was necessary in order to pull collections as new requests came up and to provide breaks for staff.

During our initial planning for BOL, we realized we needed to provide exceptions to some of our normal reading room policies. Every minute in the reading room was critical to the participants, so we worked to increase our efficiency and streamline tasks, like pulling collections. Usually, the NAA does not pull material in advance for researchers, but the amount of material requested plus the limited time researchers had with the collections warranted this exception. We also made an exception to our policy of allowing only one folder out of a box and one box on the table at a time. Researchers needed to review multiple documents from different collections to translate material or produce a comparative study. At times, this exception made monitoring the reading rooms more complicated. However, we needed to be flexible to encourage the collaborative spirit of language revitalization research. The three reading rooms were a buzz of intense activity during the afternoons.

Every research team presented their research at a final symposium open to archives staff and other invited guests. These presentations encapsulated the team's experience at BOL. All presentations were tremendously creative. For instance, one team created a cartoon in their recovered language, while another group created a video for language instruction. Many teams sang traditional songs or songs composed in their language. Others spoke about their plans and goals for bringing research and knowledge back to their communities. We felt extremely fortunate to attend these deeply personal presentations.

RESULTS

We panicked a bit at first when we learned that we would need to support the sixty researchers that BOL would bring to our archives. However, with some creativity and planning, we were able to tackle the logistical challenges that it posed to our staff of five and our usual processes. We learned how to expand our resources by drawing on and leveraging existing grant-funded projects, intern opportunities, building facilities, and reference workflows. Based on these experiences, we now have a better understanding of our physical capacity as well as our abilities to meet researchers' needs and challenges through careful consideration and practical planning.

Although we had not anticipated it, part of what made working with BOL rewarding for all of us was that each researcher had a deeply personal motivation for attending and, as a result, often experienced personal connections to the archival language material. We routinely heard comments like "Here's a picture of my grandmother" or "I never knew what that word meant. My great-uncle used to say it all the time" or "My mother's auntie is singing the song in this recording." All NAA staff and our interns were impressed by the learning, interpreting, and collaboration occurring in the reading rooms. On the final day of research, many participants expressed a profound sense of appreciation for all of our hard work. Some even hugged us and cried tears of gratitude.

Our experience with BOL was a demanding one, drawing upon all of our archival learning and knowledge of our collections, but in return the experience heavily underscored the reason we became archivists: to not only preserve and create access to records of enduring value but also to help people connect with archival manuscripts. While an intangible result, the feelings of satisfaction and pride we all felt after BOL were immeasurable and the direct result of connecting passionate researchers with our collections. As archivists, we often focus on creating and maintaining links between archival objects. The Breath of Life Institute forced us to create an environment where a large group of researchers could forge personal and meaningful interactions with our archival collections.

LESSONS LEARNED

When we decided to host BOL, we accepted the challenge and welcomed it as an opportunity to expand our services beyond what we thought was possible. But there were definitely times when BOL felt impossible. We didn't have enough space for sixty researchers. We didn't have enough tables or power outlets for laptops or chairs. There was no way that sixty people could handle some of our most fragile and significant pieces in our collection for multiple days. How would we control access? At times, it felt easier to limit our involvement with the project, limit the number of researchers into the reading rooms, and limit the number of available collections. But we realized that if we kept limiting just because it was easier, we were also limiting our impact and falling short on our mission to facilitate access to our archival collections.

In some ways, it was the very purpose of BOL that pushed us to figure out how to accommodate its needs. The institute shares the same goals for which the NAA was founded: to encourage language revitalization work and return traditional cultural knowledge back to the source communities. Our support of BOL allowed us to accept the challenges of collection access, low staffing, and lack of space and creatively identify solutions. We discovered that if you want to support a project, you would go to great lengths to make it happen. If you are tasked to work on a project that you don't support, those same challenges seem impossible, and you aren't as willing to work toward a solution.

For us, the most important step toward a solution was to ask for help. Before BOL we had no experience and no existing infrastructure to accommodate a large research group at the archives. Our resources prohibited such activity. In order to host BOL, we quickly realized that we would need outside help. We continually asked for assistance at every stage of planning and even during the actual BOL research visits. We asked the BOL organizers to fund the digitization process and an intern position. We asked our NAA colleagues to assist in the reading rooms and asked our Smithsonian colleagues for use of their space. We asked for help to identify collections for digitization and asked our interns to complete a variety of important tasks. It is amazing how much people are willing to help if you just ask. There is no way that we would have been able to host BOL without outside assistance.

We also asked participants for their patience and understanding about our less-than-ideal reading rooms, our limited microfilm readers, and so forth. During our orientations we told participants that we have never had sixty researchers visit our archives at once. We were open about the fact that BOL was a learning opportunity for us. Because we were honest with participants about our shortcomings, we felt that they were more understanding when faced with challenges like having to wait to see an original manuscript because another team was using it or having to work in a conference room with limited power outlets and low lighting. We were also careful to be as transparent as possible with our reading room policies and regulations. We explained why we asked that gloves be worn when handing photographs and described the importance of original order. We did this to create a welcoming atmosphere in our reading rooms where participants felt wanted and comfortable and to build a relationship of mutual respect not only between ourselves and participants but also between participants and collection material.

Fostering this atmosphere of mutual respect was particularly important for this group of researchers. For many BOL participants, the archives may be seen as an institution still situated within the hostile value system that first appropriated their cultural information. A number of our language resources were created under conditions fraught with power disparities. Therefore, our reference interactions need to be extremely respectful, welcoming, and intentional. The NAA is committed to responding, as best as we can, to community concerns about respectful management of collection material. We created a number of "Information Please" forms, where we make note of corrections or additions to our catalog records and finding aids. Many of the BOL participants were extremely knowledgeable about the nature of the information contained in our archives. Therefore, they corrected misspellings of family names or towns or of wrongly identified individuals. We used this information to update our finding aids and catalog records.

As we mentioned previously, the *Protocols for Native American Archival Materials* were extremely helpful with training our interns. The *Protocols* also provided us with guidance on how to encourage cooperation and dialogue with Native American researchers. It was important to us to establish relationships with the members of each Native American community who visited the NAA as part of BOL. We not only wanted to encourage future use of our collection but also to learn about how these members viewed our collection material and archival policies. The *Protocols* discuss in length the benefits of cross-cultural trainings for archivists and Native American communities.

CONCLUSION

The Breath of Life Institute was a wonderful opportunity for the NAA. It created a number of challenges for us but also inspired us to develop useful solutions. In addition to challenging our preconceptions about the limitations of our ability to provide reference services, BOL enabled us to improve other aspects of how we provide access. To support BOL we created numerous digital surrogates—over a thousand pages of manuscript material—to allow unprecedented access to a variety of manuscripts. We added these images to our online catalog to expand access even further. As a result of our research into our own archival collections, we now have a better understanding of our significant language holdings.

In June 2013 the Breath of Life Archival Institute for Indigenous Languages returned to the NAA. Our planning and hard work for the 2011 institute provided a solid blueprint for how we would host the 2013 institute. We were again able to fund two interns through BOL and SIMA, and this time we added a third intern with funding from the SAT grant. We also used two satellite reading rooms, identified and digitized relevant material, and distributed it on flash drives. We successfully multiplied our space, our collections, and ourselves. We look forward to the next BOL, when we will again, for a short time, go forth and multiply. Our plan for BOL could be easily adopted to host any large group of researchers at the NAA.

While useful on a practical level, our work with these researchers provided us with even more meaningful experiences. These people connected deeply with our collections. Some heard the voice of a long-deceased relative in an audio recording or read the words written by a great-great-great-grandfather in an old journal. Copies of these manuscripts and recordings were taken back to their source communities and experienced a second life outside of the archives. A number of the BOL participants used their research from the NAA to create curricula to revitalize their native languages. We hope that this is just the beginning of long working relationships with these researchers and their communities.

On a more personal level, we can't think of another research group that would bring such excitement and energy into our reading room. The enthusiasm for archival research displayed by the BOL participants was contagious and uplifting. These researchers also shared their knowledge with us, helping us to better understand our collections—both in small ways, by correcting our cataloging information, and in big ways, by reminding us of the role these materials can play in their source communities. Our experiences have reminded us not to run away in the face of a challenge but to embrace that challenge and find creative ways to provide even greater access.

Leanda Gahegan is librarian at the Charlotte Mecklenburg Library. Until 2012 she was the reference archivist at the National Anthropological Archives, Smithsonian Institution. Gina Rappaport is photo archivist and head archivist at the National Anthropological Archives, Smithsonian Institution.

SEVEN

The Right Tool at the Right Time

Implementing Responsive Reproduction Policies and Procedures

Melanie Griffin and Matthew Knight, University of South Florida

Like many medium-sized special collections departments housed in university libraries, the University of South Florida's (USF) special collections department has recently faced a number of challenges brought about by shrinking staff, dwindling budgets, and rising researcher expectations. As a result, we have reevaluated workflows in order to work smarter and provide the same level of service with fewer resources. One area in particular that we intensively investigated was the department's reproduction policies, procedures, and equipment needs, both for in-person and distance researchers.

Long-standing policy required that department staff mediate each reproduction request and charge a fee for all but the most nominal photocopy orders. This workflow proved expensive and time consuming for all involved due to the staff time required to fill requests, bill requests, and collect payment. In fact, while analyzing our policies and procedures, we discovered that it cost far more in staff time to bill a copy request than we recovered by charging a fee. The system also often resulted in a lengthy wait for patrons and was incompatible with interlibrary loan (ILL) procedures already in place in the library. In addition, we frequently had to deny requests due to the fragility of bound items and the department's equipment limitations. The flatbed photocopier available for our use was less than ideal for bound items, and the only way to provide patrons with reproductions that did not damage the original was to refer them to the library's digitization on-demand service, which was prohibitively expensive for most users, especially students.

At the same time that the department began reassessing its reproduction policies and procedures, we noticed that many of the researchers making use of our collections were also working in departments with shrinking staff and dwindling budgets, resulting in shorter research trips and significantly smaller amounts of institutional support for reproduction fees. One outcome was the rising frequency of time-pressed researchers making manual transcriptions of materials in our collections as a result of our inability to provide access to photocopies or digital scans of materials. Because of the shifting needs of researchers and the department's reduced resources, we decided to formally evaluate our reproduction policies and procedures and to seek creative solutions to budgetary limitations, with the ultimate goal of increasing access to and use of our collections.

PLANNING

Anecdotal evidence had, for quite some time, suggested to reading room staff that our reproduction policies were problematic for all of our users, not just visiting researchers. In the spring of 2011, we launched a formal, department-wide assessment strategy that, in part, sought to quantify the patron experience in the reading room and highlight areas for possible improvement. While we permitted the use of digital cameras in the reading room and provided a limited number of photocopies free of charge, the lack of adequate, efficient, and affordable reproduction services was high on the list of patron-perceived problems, and this data proved instrumental in our implementation process.

Inspired by the principles of responsive web design, which seeks to provide the optimal viewing experience regardless of the platform used to access the site, USF special collections wanted to provide optimal reproduction services to the widest array of users possible, regardless of a patron's location or the type of materials requested for reproduction. While discussing possibilities for a complete fix, we implemented a short-term solution to help alleviate the problem. The department had long allowed patrons to use their own digital cameras, and we began allowing the use of personal portable scanners, provided that staff first checked the condition of materials and their suitability for use on the available equipment. We also provided patrons who did not bring their own equipment with access to a small, handheld digital camera for unmediated—but supervised—use in the reading room. The digital camera was better than nothing for patrons but not by much. The resolution and potential for blurry images from a handheld, flash-free camera proved particularly problematic for patrons wishing to reproduce textual materials, especially in tightly bound volumes. In addition to being less than perfect, this short-term solution also did nothing to address the needs of researchers at a distance.

Our staff members discussed a variety of possible approaches for a long-term solution, including:

- Increasing the number of photocopies provided to patrons and simultaneously lifting charges for student, faculty, and not-for-profit use. This potential solution addressed two concerns with previous policies: cost for researchers and cost for the institution, as the bulk of the institution's cost was in staff time spent on the billing process. This approach did not provide a solution for ILL requests or bound materials.
- Increasing digitization on-demand services, with all reproduction requests being routed through the digital collections and services unit. Although this approach would have allowed the department to fill any reproduction request, regardless of format or binding, it would have required revisiting the pricing structure of digitization on demand. It would also have shifted the burden of mediating requests and creating facsimiles to another understaffed unit, resulting in increased operating costs.
- Encouraging use of digital cameras and ceasing all photocopy and digitization on-demand requests. Of all approaches discussed, this was deemed the least desirable, as it further restricted access to reproductions rather than offering an improved service.
- Installing a scanner with a book cradle in the reading room, thereby allowing researchers to make their own reproductions. This solution had the potential of solving the widest range of existing problems, including limiting staff time devoted to reproductions, widening the types of materials that were eligible for reproduction, and allowing staff to make use of the equipment to facilitate the fulfillment of ILL requests via the creation of quick, in-house scans.

This final approach was the most attractive to our department, as it would permit patrons to be more self-sufficient and for staff to increase the types of ILL and distance-researcher requests that we were able to fill. In order to implement the policy, we identified a number of potential hurdles, the largest of which was purchasing a new scanner.

As we first revisited our reproduction policies partly in response to budget and staffing cuts, we knew that getting a request for new equipment filled through normal channels would not be feasible. Instead, we partnered with librarians in the access services unit (USF's name for its circulation department) on a collaborative student technology fee grant proposal to fund the purchase of three Bookeye scanners, one of which would be housed in the special collections reading room. The grant proposal, submitted in March 2011, stated that the ability of USF students and faculty to convert print-only materials to a digital format is critical to scholarly communications, research, and learning. Because many of the library's most useful and valuable materials are unable to leave the building and there are inadequate and ineffective on-site means for patrons to convert these print materials to a high-resolution, portable, digital format, there is limited access to knowledge contained in the library's collections. It was therefore recommended that a state-of-the-art digital scanning system be placed in strategic areas of the library: the special collections reading room, the periodicals area, and the map and reference collection area.

The grant proposal was a success, and the scanner was purchased and placed in a publicly accessible area of our reading room in January 2012. We created a banner that reads "Free Scanner! Use Me!" to encourage patron use, and when queried about photocopies, all staff were trained to inform patrons that, while photocopies were no longer available, self-service scans were free.

IMPLEMENTATION

The Bookeye 4 Color Planetary Book scanner acquired by special collections offers a number of useful features for our staff and patrons, including the ability to send scans to an e-mail account or save them to a USB device; a 120° "V" cradle mode to protect bindings and spines; the capability to scan at preservation-quality 600 DPI; the choice of color, black-and-white, and gray-scale images; and the option to save files in multiple formats, making compiling and reviewing files more convenient. The scanner has since been upgraded to allow patrons to send files to cloud storage or scan a QR code to retrieve their files from a temporary URL. The scanner can also accommodate items up to seventeen by twenty-four inches, a vast improvement over the flatbed photocopier that could not handle large maps or many of our bound monographs. An interactive touch screen offers a simple, user-friendly interface with an electronic keyboard, and the LCD display screen provides a convenient preview of the scanned items. Users also have the ability to crop and edit images before they are saved and sent.

Each user must accept a copyright agreement before the scanning session is initiated; once the terms are accepted, the process can begin. The scanner has two modes of operation: simple and advanced. The simple function defaults to a resolution of 200 DPI and saves files in PDF format; this option works well for inexperienced users or for those just requiring one or two basic scans. The advanced mode allows much more flexibility for the user, including the ability to name folders, scan up to 600 DPI, choose from a wider selection of scan areas, and output files in a variety of formats. We routinely suggest that patrons utilize the advanced settings to achieve the best possible results. The image resolution, color mode, brightness, contrast, and scanning area can be changed at any time during the scanning process, including at the final "Save or Send" stage. Finally, there is a convenient guide tab on the interactive touch screen that offers step-by-step instructions for scanning, saving, and sending materials.

Our official reproduction policy, available on our website and as part of the user agreement that all patrons acknowledge during the reader registration process, now reads:

> We offer a variety of options for providing reproductions of our materials. Patrons may take pictures with their personal cameras and cell phones, though the camera's flash may not be used. We also offer a self-service Bookeye scanner, which allows files to be saved to a patron's USB drive or cloud storage or e-mailed directly from the scanner. We no longer provide photocopies.
>
> A staff member must approve all requests to photograph, scan, or otherwise reproduce materials. Staff reserves the right to refuse any digital reproduction request for copyright or preservation purposes. Please see below for additional information on copyright.

The policy intentionally does not limit the number of scans that a patron may make; a separate policy governs copyright and reminds users that they are responsible for abiding by applicable laws, especially those governing fair use. To date, we have noticed no increase in workload for staff to approve all reproductions. Materials are routinely examined for condition before they are given to patrons, and we encourage desk staff to communicate restrictions on photographing or scanning materials when they are first provided to researchers.

Our largest concern with providing patrons with the ability to make unlimited scans was that we were able to purchase only one scanner; we worried that long lines might prevent all patrons from making use of the equipment. We decided to implement an informal, collegial policy that allowed users to scan all that they would like, provided that they played nicely with other patrons who were waiting in line. We were pleasantly surprised to find that this informal policy works well the vast majority of the time and that most patrons are more than willing to wait in line for the opportunity to receive free reproductions.

Delivering these new and improved services did require institutional buy-in for a reproduction policy that eliminated fee structures for student, staff, faculty, and not-for-profit use of any kind, including publication. Our approach to gaining institutional support for changing the fee structure associated with reproduction requests was twofold. First, we emphasized the use of student technology fee funds to support the purchase of the scanner. As students had, in a sense, already paid for the acquisition of the equipment, we wanted to avoid double charging them for its use. Second, we performed a cost/benefit analysis of recent reproduction requests and were able to illustrate how it actually cost the library more to process the modest fee payments than it did to complete the requests themselves. For both reasons, administration supported our decision to establish a new, largely free pricing structure. Reproduction requests for commercial use, however, are assessed a fee and are dealt with on an ad-hoc basis by the digital collections and services unit. Updating these reproduction policies has increased our ability to provide both our on-site and distance patrons with more streamlined access to our collections.

Of course, in addition to better serving the needs of our on-site patrons, the implementation of a scanner was intended to give us greater flexibility in providing access to materials to off-site patrons and fulfilling special, distance, and ILL requests. In terms of workflow, all of these kinds of requests are routed to the department's operations manager. This approach allows for consistency and efficiency, and it simplifies the channels of communication between staff and patrons. Requests can be delivered by the ILL staff, received through our online contact form, made over the phone, or sent in e-mail correspondence; therefore, having one person as the main contact made the most sense in our situation. Requests are dealt with upon receipt, and the turnaround time is generally same day, depending on the details of the request. With that said, patrons are normally told that they can expect their requests delivered within three business days. This protects against unexpected staff absences or the odd request that comes in at 5:00 p.m. on a Friday afternoon.

In the case of ILL, these requests tended to be denied out of hand in the past, as our ILL department did not handle special collections–to–special collections loans on a routine basis, and the fragility of materials did not allow for reproduction on the photocopier. Now, although an auto-deflection program eliminates more than 50 percent of patron requests for monographic materials via ILL, requests for articles or fragile materials can be fulfilled. Materials are scanned at 300 DPI in gray scale, unless otherwise specified, and saved as a PDF. The files are then sent to the ILL department through regular e-mail or by using Dropbox if the file size is exceedingly large. Special requests are tailored to the patron's needs and are either delivered by e-mail, Dropbox link, or a temporary URL, depending on the size of the reproduced file. Initially, we considered saving copies of some of these requests for use in our online digital collections; however, while the Bookeye scanner does produce quality overhead scans, it cannot consistently produce results that meet the quality standards for presentation in our online collections. Further, the unstructured and inconsistent nature of these requests inhibits strategic collection development. That said, we do save copies of special and ILL requests in the event that they are duplicated in the future.

In 2008, special collections had also implemented Aeon, a request and workflow management system that allows patrons to request items directly from the online catalog for viewing in the department's reading room. Recently, Aeon has incorporated a photo-duplication module into its software; this new feature has a customizable workflow and can be configured to incorporate a billing process should we choose to charge for certain reproduction services in the future. The module also allows staff to track the status of the item being digitized and the copy itself through the same transaction number, which keeps the process simple and efficient. We have been exploring the potential in this photo-duplication component and expect full implementation in the near future. Aeon developers also created an add-on for us that links Knowledge Tracker, our licensed reference management system that routes online requests to the proper faculty member, to the Aeon interface for improved functionality.

RESULTS

The new policies and equipment paid immediate dividends for our on-site patrons. Unlike the previous photocopying service, which required a staff member to make a limited number of copies and then charge for any additional items, the scanner now allows for self-sufficiency on the part of the researcher and enables a freer, more expansive reproduction policy: If you can scan it and are not violating copyright law, go for it. The positive response from our users was overwhelming; students were thrilled to be able to send scans directly to their e-mail accounts, and faculty and community users marveled at the high-quality scans and began to abandon their preference for photocopies. A visitor from a research university was especially pleased to be able to scan multiple items at no cost. She even sent a follow-up e-mail that not only thanked us for our help during her visit but also asked how we managed to convince the administration to support a no-fee policy for reproduction. She is now working on changing the reproduction policies at her home institution.

It also did not take long before we noticed positive results from our new policies for researchers at a distance. Shortly after implementation, a call came from our ILL department asking us to handle a patron request from New Jersey. Apparently, this individual had been repeatedly calling over a long period of time trying to acquire a copy of a dime novel in our collection through ILL; however, as the item was published in 1878 on highly acidic paper, a physical transfer was not advisable due to its instability, and the item was far too fragile to place on the photocopier. Therefore, under our old policies, this request was repeatedly denied, and with USF being one of only two libraries in the United States on record as owning this item, the patron was left with only two choices: pay for a digital reproduction or give up her opportunity to acquire the item. Fortunately, now there was another option. Our overhead scanner was able to digitize the delicate book without difficulty, but the file was too large to send via e-mail, so we uploaded the file to Dropbox and e-mailed the link to the patron. She was absolutely thrilled and wrote the following in reply: "I have been trying to get a copy of this novel for over two years. It means so much to me as the protagonist in the book was based on my great-great grandfather and his adventures in Ireland. Words cannot express my gratitude to you and the University. Thank you for taking the time and effort to make a wish come true."

Just a few days later, an alumna called to say that her Ph.D. thesis was destroyed in a house fire, and as she had completed the dissertation in the 1980s, she had no other physical or electronic copy. Given that the fees for reproducing a bound thesis are rather exorbitant, the patron asked if there was anything that could be done. Because USF special collections holds an archival copy of all master's and Ph.D. theses in storage, her dissertation was quickly retrieved and scanned at 300 DPI with the Bookeye, and a Dropbox link to the file was sent to the patron. The entire transaction was completed within an hour of the patron's initial request, much to her surprise and delight. Under the former policies, she would have had to fill out a special reproduction request, send it to us, and pay the assessed fee for a non-USF-affiliated researcher of twenty-five dollars per page. Alternatively, she could have received photocopies for twenty cents per page, which would have added considerable staff time to the process and would have produced a low-quality result.

The acquisition of the new scanner did not only benefit patrons and ILL staff, but it also proved a perfect tool for completing in-house projects that did not necessarily need to be executed by the digital collections and services unit or that benefit our patrons but did not align with institutional digitization priorities. In the past, items that special collections wished to digitize for presentations, displays, or other projects would need to leave the department, thereby subjecting them to another unit's schedule and workflow. With the Bookeye in house, we are able to digitize quickly rare and delicate items safely and at a high resolution—especially items that are too fragile to be laid flat and scanned or photographed.

For example, special collections holds a two-volume journal written by Dr. Ellis Hughes, an assistant surgeon during the Second Seminole War (1835–1842). Representatives from the Fort Lauderdale Historical Society had long desired for us to make the diaries available online, as travel to and from Tampa to consult the volumes was not convenient or even possible for many interested users. With our new scanner in place, in the fall of 2012, we decided to take this opportunity to digitize the diaries and make them available through our online catalog. While we normally do not use the overhead scanner to digitize materials for our online collections, as the results are not of the same high quality that a book-edge scanner might provide, the fragility of the material precluded using flatbed equipment, and great care was taken to maximize the appearance of the diary for researchers. So, in this particular case, the importance of the diaries to distance users outweighed our normally strict quality controls. Within a week the diaries were scanned and edited, and within two weeks they were available online for researchers everywhere.

An unanticipated but very welcome result of the new policies in special collections was the positive impact on our outreach efforts to other departments and faculty on campus. Since the purchase of the new scanner, librarians have been able to collaborate more fully and frequently with teaching faculty to incorporate digital projects into the curriculum. One example of this type of collaboration occurred in an upper-level American literature course offered in the spring 2013 semester that was built around USF's dime novel collection. Instead of requiring students to write a traditional term paper, the instructor had her students work in groups to produce online exhibitions built in Omeka. A special collections librarian provided the reference and instructional support associated with a traditional course requiring extensive use of our materials. In addition, the librarian also offered the students instruction for best practices in the creation of digital surrogates using the new overhead scanner, enabling them to create the objects and files needed for their online exhibitions. We were initially nervous about a class of undergraduates, most of whom had never visited a special collections department or archives before the course began, handling a collection comprised of extremely fragile, acidic materials so extensively and for reformatting purposes, but we discovered that the benefit of student engagement far outweighed the minor wear and tear to the materials. Careful instruction and supervision ensured proper handling of materials, resulting in the success of a new course that will be offered again in coming semesters.

After the new policies had been in place for a semester, we repeated the reading room user satisfaction survey that originally identified increased access to reproduction services as a patron need. By using the same instrument, we were able to assess the success of our new policies, ensure consistent data, and not introduce new variables. Results were largely positive, with 86 percent of users strongly agreeing or agreeing that "Duplication services met my needs," as opposed to 63 percent under the old policies. Open-ended responses to the survey tended to be equally positive, with patrons expressing their enthusiasm for the reduced cost of their research trips as well as the ability to make reproductions at the point of need instead of waiting for staff to have the time to make photocopies and mail them to the requester's home or office. A few comments suggested, however, that regardless of circumstances, all patrons would never find duplication policies and services completely amenable. Some patrons, for example, missed photocopies; others were nonplussed by the self-service nature of our duplication policy for on-site researchers. On one occasion a patron was dismayed that we have only one scanner and that other patrons needed to be offered the opportunity to use the equipment. These and other similar complaints have been few and far between, and given the overall positive reception we have received to the new policies and equipment, we have decided to take them with the proverbial grain of salt while also seeking ways to make our policies more transparent and user friendly. The complaint about the single scanner, for example, led to modified staff training in which we emphasize to reading room desk attendants the necessity for making sure that patrons are aware that they must take turns with the equipment.

During initial discussions about implementing policies that would eliminate fees for the majority of reproduction requests, we were concerned for the potential of abuse of the system, especially by distance researchers hoping to avoid a research trip entirely. Under the old fee structures, reproduction requests rapidly became cost prohibitive, resulting in very few requests for substantial duplication of materials. We were not certain, however, whether the lack of requests for mass photocopies or digitization was a direct result of the fee structure because the majority of patrons who requested reproductions were unfamiliar with our policies and the documents describing prices for various services. With a lack of data to inform the discussion, we decided to offer free reproductions for education, research, and not-for-profit use and to reassess after six months (or sooner, if needed). After implementation, we were pleased that there were only one or two patrons who appeared to be trying to take unfair advantage of our more generous reproduction services. Other than that, we have not observed users, upon learning that there would be no charge for digital scans, increase copy orders or return at a later date with exorbitant requests. We still receive roughly the same number of requests that we are unable to fill under the new policies as we did under the old, fee-driven model. The conversations we have with patrons who have requested reproduction orders that we are unable to fill remain unchanged, with staff explaining why we are unable to provide a digital copy of a complete monograph that is under copyright or a scan of every page in a 250-box archival collection that includes an individual's name rather than focusing on the cost of filling such a request. In regards to ILL requests, statistics show a slight decrease in the number of canceled requests since we implemented the new policy and scanner.

The reaction to our new policies from patrons and library staff has been largely positive. After all, patrons are able to scan multiple images free of charge, and library staff need no longer refuse certain requests or enforce rigid payment structures. Also, the ability to send completed scans to e-mail accounts or cloud storage has made the digitization process much more convenient for researchers. Our out-of-town patrons have been especially pleased with the new policies, as requests for copies can now be fulfilled almost immediately through e-mail rather than having to wait weeks for photocopies to arrive via standard delivery.

LESSONS LEARNED

Although the scanner we purchased is advertised as simple and easy to use, we discovered that there is a decided learning curve involved to achieve the best scans possible, requiring the need for more staff training than anticipated. Further, as many of our patrons are uncomfortable with newer technologies, it required some finessing to convince them that the new scanner was a better alternative to the more familiar, if inherently flawed, photocopier.

The installation of our new overhead scanner has undoubtedly improved workflow and increased patron satisfaction, but it is not without its liabilities. For example, image quality is inferior to that achieved by a flatbed or book-edge scanner; this generally does not create an issue in our department, but sometimes patrons who require a high-quality image are disappointed in the result. Further, the hardware itself can cause problems: two lasers and the unit's hard drive were replaced within the first year of use, and frequent recalibrations to the software are necessary. Thus, an extended warranty for equipment like this is strongly recommended. That said, even knowing what we know now, we would likely purchase the same type of overhead scanner again. The simplicity of use, speed of operation, and safe-handling features still make it a solid choice for our operation.

When we first acquired the overhead scanner and implemented the new, self-service policies for users in the reading room, we experienced a limited amount of push-back from patrons who were accustomed to our previous practices. Our own excitement for the new equipment, coupled with enthusiasm for a mechanism by which patrons could make the reproductions that they needed without damaging our materials or incurring additional costs, led us to implement the self-serve policy and eliminate photocopies immediately. In retrospect, an official grace period with both policies and services available simultaneously would probably have been beneficial. As it turned out, we ultimately had to create an ad-hoc photocopy grace period to make limited photocopies for some of our most technologically resistant patrons. Having a clearly articulated policy about the phasing out of photocopies would have resulted in more transparent expectations, both for staff and users.

CONCLUSION

Although the impetus for revisiting and subsequently revising our department's reproduction policies was unpleasant budget cuts and staff reductions, the process ultimately led to positive outcomes, the most significant of which is allowing us to better serve our patrons' needs. The solution we reached is customized to USF's institutional culture, the demographics of the department's user population, and our staffing levels. A single scanner, for example, is sufficient for our reading room needs, and given budget and staffing reductions, it was crucial that we find a reproduction policy that shifted most work from staff to patrons.

Although our particular environment led to new policies and procedures that may not be tenable for other departments, the guiding principles are extensible. First, the availability of new technology inspired us to rethink how we handled reproduction requests and to stop doing things the way that we had always done them just because that was the way they had always been done. Routine reassessment of reproduction policies enables archives and special collections to make thoughtful, proactive choices that best serve the department and the department's users. Second, institutional buy-in is crucial. Framing proposed modifications in language that mirrors the parent institution's strategic goals can be particularly beneficial. In our case, we emphasized the impact of free scans for students because USF is in the midst of a student success campaign. Third, the inclusion of relevant statistics to support proposed policy changes can prove key in discussions with administrators, demonstrating data-driven decision making. Our old reproduction policies cost both our department as well as the library's business office more to implement than they recouped, and our ability to propose a data-driven decision was instrumental in securing support for abandoning a policy that, superficially, appeared that it would make money for the university. Finally, a willingness to explore a range of possible solutions is crucial. At the outset of our policy revisions, we generated a list of potential solutions, ranging from the good to the ideal. Implementing the ideal solution immediately was not feasible due to budget limitations, but having a variety of options on the table enabled us to make smaller, interim changes that positively benefited both our department and our researchers.

Implicit in the USF special collections service model is the knowledge that our policies must develop over time as the needs of our patrons change. The redesign of our reproduction policies gave us the opportunity to explore the wants and needs of our community of users. By balancing those wants and needs with institutional concerns, we were able to implement an inclusive and successful policy for our students, faculty, and community users. Over a short time span, this policy has led to positive changes for our patrons, enabling us to increase anytime, anywhere access to many items in our collections.

Melanie Griffin is the special collections librarian and *Matthew Knight* is the coordinator of special collections at University of South Florida.

EIGHT

Going Mobile

Using iPads to Improve the Reading Room Experience

Cheryl Oestreicher, Julia Stringfellow, and Jim Duran, Boise State University

In 2010 Boise State University launched a three-year mobile-learning initiative to utilize mobile technology in the classroom to facilitate learning. Through courses, programs, and faculty preparation, the initiative's goals included increasing student engagement in learning, developing digital literacy skills, and producing "technology-mediated innovations in content delivery and creation."[1] Faculty and students participated from a variety of disciplines, including arts, humanities, sciences, business, education, engineering, health sciences, and social science.

The initial role of the university's Albertsons Library in the program was to provide students access to mobile devices, e-books, and other e-content (such as streaming video). In fall 2012, the library expanded its use of mobile technology when Boise State implemented University Foundations (UF) curriculum for new students. The library conducts instruction sessions for all UF courses and facilitates students working in groups and using iPads to practice and learn research skills and strategies. This active learning approach is effective and not only helps students learn, but also often it is the first time some students have used an iPad, thus they are also introduced to a new form of technology.

To facilitate use and knowledge of mobile technology and therefore be better able to provide resources to students and faculty, the library administration purchased iPads for all staff. The special collections and archives staff were part of this mobile-learning initiative, and our own use of the library-provided iPads as well our experience with UF instruction naturally inspired us to discuss how we could use mobile technology to better serve our patrons. This case study explores our experience providing iPads for patron use in our reading room, including how we established our baseline policies and processes, how researchers have received and used the new technology, and our reflections on our future plans.

PLANNING

The library's special collections and archives (SCA) consists of four staff that includes three library faculty (the head of SCA and two archivists/ librarians) and one professional position (an archives associate). We have two main collecting areas: university records and local history of Boise and southwest Idaho. Of more than 475 reference requests for archival material for fiscal year 2013, faculty, staff, and students represented approximately 55 percent of inquiries, with community and others making up the other 45 percent. Community and other patrons include non–Boise State professors and students, alumni, local authors, journalists, documentary filmmakers, television producers, donors and their descendants, community organizations, and others primarily from the United States but also Canada, Australia, Germany, Japan, and England.

SCA wanted to participate in wider library efforts to increase use of mobile technology, and using iPads in the reading room was the obvious choice. The library already made iPads available for circulation to students and use in library instruction, so the mobile devices were already readily available to us. Therefore, utilizing iPads as opposed to other devices (e.g., iTouch or other tablets) aligned us with already-established library programs.

The library has about sixty iPads available for UF instruction sessions. After the completion of UF instruction, about nine weeks into the semester, SCA received permission to borrow four iPads for the reading room. Because each of us already had personal iPads supplied by the library, we were all familiar with the technology and did not need any additional training. Overall, the technology for supporting our iPad use was largely behind the scenes and away from researchers and primarily involved adding apps and reimaging the devices.

The SCA staff individually downloaded and experimented with various apps on our personal iPads, such as ones for file sharing and photo documentation, to test their appropriateness for our researchers. To decide which apps to permanently install on our patron iPads, we considered as many potential uses as possible. We then met as a group and decided on a final list and ended up with just a handful of apps. It was agreed that file sharing was an essential feature for our users, so we added the Google Drive app (although we later switched to Dropbox, as we discuss later). We all looked at free photography apps but decided to just use the standard iPad camera app because it was supported by many other default features. Some of the third-party photo apps were impressive, and we'll continue to watch for improvements with syncing to e-mail and cloud storage. We also selected an app called Magnify HD that displayed a magnified camera shot, which we thought patrons could use instead of traditional magnifying instruments. We expected that having extra magnification would help researchers scrutinize hard-to-read documents and maps, and it also complies with the Society of American Archivists' (SAA) "Best Practices for Working with Archives Researchers with Physical Disabilities."[2] We purposely started with only a few apps to keep things simple for us and for users, and we plan to add more as researchers' needs expand.

We first tried to load these apps on the patron iPads with our personal Apple accounts. While our accounts were used only for free apps, this procedure produced sustainability problems that we hadn't anticipated. Apps installed using personal accounts could not be deleted, updated, or modified without the owner's password. The use of personal accounts was also a security issue; if the user did not log out, there was potential for unauthorized access or installation. After some time and discussion with the library IT unit, we decided to have IT install new applications using a library administration Apple account, which was later replaced with their reimaging process.

For routine updates for the circulating and instruction iPads, our IT department had already implemented a system of reimaging using Apple Configurator. We worked with IT to develop a default profile for the SCA iPads, which includes home-screen icons for our finding aids database; library website; SCA website; CONTENTdm digital collections; and ScholarWorks, our institutional repository. With this default profile in place, SCA staff can periodically reimage the iPads back to our default settings—keeping storage at a maximum, removing viruses or bugs, and ensuring apps and software are updated regularly. We considered several options for how often to reimage the iPads, including after every researcher, once a day, and once a week. The reimaging process takes place on a different floor than SCA, so it is not always practical to complete after every researcher. We are conscious that researchers may log in to websites or e-mail using personal information that should be deleted after each use, but there are days when iPads are not used by any patrons. Over time, we will establish firm procedures after we have more knowledge of patron use patterns.

Of course, security is a concern with mobile devices. We were concerned that patrons might walk off with iPads, either accidentally or intentionally. While the majority of the time there are only one to three researchers in our reference room, which is reasonable for staff to monitor, there can be more when there are classes or groups using the archives. For example, there are kinesiology classes that require class time for research, meaning there could be fifteen to thirty students at one time.

We first considered attaching the iPads to the tables in the research room, either by adhering them directly to the table or attaching a cord to allow for some mobility. The former meant they were no longer mobile, and the latter posed other issues, including not being able to have the iPads in protective cases due to the cord/lock mechanism and also having to unlock them to recharge. Neither option supported the idea of "mobile" devices and had the potential for more problems rather than solutions. Another argument against tethering the iPads is that this doesn't allow patrons to easily take pictures of materials; limited mobility could make this difficult and would impact the quality of the images. Additionally, when patrons had questions about viewing resources on the iPads, we thought it would be very handy for them to bring the iPad directly over to the desk staff for assistance.

We then considered not putting iPads on the tables but keeping them at the desk and asking patrons to leave a form of identification at the desk while using one—essentially they would be "checked out" for use. We rejected this idea because it meant we had to ask every patron if they wanted to use them, requiring another procedure for both staff and the public. We also predicted that they would not be used as much if they were not readily available. If patrons chose not to take one, we doubted they would come back and ask if they changed their mind. Instead, we left them out on the tables, encouraged their use, and often used them to start reference interviews. After we began making the iPads available, we observed that some patrons did not use them immediately but would after some time had passed. Giving patrons the freedom to choose when they used the iPad without extra paperwork or procedures increased the use of the devices. It was ultimately decided that having a staff member at the reference desk keeping an eye on the use of research materials and iPads in the reading room was sufficient.

IMPLEMENTATION

Beginning in November 2012, we began placing our four borrowed iPads on the four reading room tables daily. Despite our earlier concerns about security, we have had no issues with them being misplaced, and leaving them freely available on the tables has fostered more use by patrons. Staff use them to show patrons finding aids, digital collections, and other resources, which encourages patrons to use both the iPad and library resources more widely on their own. Our first point of contact with researchers is at our reference desk, which is outside the reading room.

After learning the depth of the question, sometimes staff members will take an iPad off a reading room table and bring it back to the reference desk to help patrons start searching for resources. Patrons can then take the iPad into the reading room and have the finding aids or other digital content already available to continue their research.

The iPads have also been extremely helpful with class group projects. SCA hosts kinesiology students every semester, about fifteen to thirty students per class working in groups of three to five as they research aspects of university history: sports, recreation, and student activities. Having iPads available enabled students to access online resources, including images of the campus and student activities in CONTENTdm and university history books, course catalogs, and student newspapers through ScholarWorks. Accessing these online resources with iPads complemented the process of viewing physical resources, such as athletic programs and scrapbooks. Being able to easily view the online resources at the groups' tables in the reading room enabled the students to conduct their research in a more efficient manner. Students with personal laptops could take notes and work on the group's final presentation while others looked through the online resources on the iPad. Additionally, the reading room only has one public computer, so having iPads for each group meant no waiting in line.

A benefit of the kinesiology classes working in groups was that SCA staff was able to provide assistance with the iPads to groups rather than repeat steps to each individual. When a group came to SCA for the first time, part of their training on how to do research and handle materials included how to use the iPad. This involved accessing the Internet, locating the online content relevant to their topics, and other basic iPad skills. Explaining how to use the iPad about ten times instead of more than fifty times for a class was more efficient for us. The students were also able to e-mail links to themselves from the iPads for future reference.

Aligning with general library instruction, SCA staff utilized iPads for graduate and undergraduate history instruction of both library and archives resources, including the library catalog, article databases, Northwest Digital Archives (NWDA) finding aids database, and CONTENTdm collections. By borrowing additional iPads, Cheryl demonstrated techniques and resources and had each student follow along on the iPads. Many had not previously used mobile devices for library research, so some training was necessary on navigating the iPad, such as where to find the special character keys to log in to their library accounts. One snag with history instruction was using the resource Social Explorer; iPads don't have Flash, therefore students were unable to access that resource.

Students actively engaged in their own research while Cheryl demonstrated resources. As Cheryl explained search methods for NWDA, she asked students to enter search terms applicable to their projects. She then engaged the students and faculty in a discussion of what search terms were used, what resources (if any) were found, and how to strengthen searches. In one class, the professor had not yet used an iPad, so she also followed along and learned how to better navigate a mobile device.

In February 2013, Cheryl and Jim hosted a community workshop that utilized historic photos. The Boise City Department of Arts and History hosts monthly lectures that often have a workshop in conjunction. A Boise State history faculty member gave a lecture on "Memory and History: Inclusion and Exclusion in Public Commemoration" and offered a workshop to allow participants to create their own public commemoration using current and historic photographs. We provided iPads to nine participants to search our digital collections. The project was to choose a historic photo of a campus building, take a photo of the same building, and merge them together to create a "now and then" image demonstrating their interpretation of the present and past. Participants used cameras and phones to take their own photos after choosing their historic photos. With only one public access computer in the reading room, providing iPads to each person allowed them to proceed at their own pace and not be pressured for time. We also made some print photos available for research so they could see the differences between virtual and paper research. We showed them how quickly they can browse photos online instead of looking through multiple folders. Most participants had never used an iPad, and while a few were hesitant, they became more engaged as we demonstrated how to use them and as they watched others use them effectively.

Use of iPads went beyond searching our resources. Researchers use the camera to take photos of items with a paper credit line to include with each image. This saves wear and tear on materials caused by photocopying or scanning. Images from iPads are of a reasonable quality for research but not the high quality needed for reproduction or publication. All photos are saved to the preinstalled Photos app, and if an iPad's photo collection becomes cluttered, we simply reimage the device to wipe the memory clean. Patrons are responsible for letting us know if they need to copy their files from our iPads. As discussed later, we have implemented a successful solution to transferring files by using Dropbox.

Overall, providing iPads for patrons involved little staff time to implement. After our initial planning of policies and procedures and deciding which apps to load, the only staff time required is placing the iPads on the reading room tables at opening and securing them at closing. Some coordination with our IT unit was necessary to discuss security options, set up the reimaging process, and install apps. IT staff were very helpful in explaining all available options and helping provide the best and most practical solutions. The reimaging process they built only requires us to walk downstairs and plug the iPads into a laptop, and the iPads automatically reset to our default setup. Also, we found these devices stay charged for some time, often lasting over a week without requiring recharging. We have a designated spot in the staff area where they are easily plugged in to charge.

At the beginning of the project, we had to return the borrowed iPads when they were needed for instruction use. But as upgrades and staff turnover made more available, we later received three iPads for dedicated SCA use (two iPad 1s and one iPad 3). Our long-term plan is to purchase two to four iPad 3s, ideally to have one per reading room table.

RESULTS

Adding iPads to the reading room was well received by all archives staff, library administration, and researchers. Library administration recognized the benefits of having iPads in the reading room and supported all efforts to make this happen. They particularly appreciated SCA staff working to align the unit within the larger library mobile-learning initiatives.

We have found iPads are an easy way to connect patrons to finding aids and other online resources. When assisting patrons in the reading room, we use iPads to answer their questions without having to go back to desks or other computers. By using iPads instead of desktops, patrons are less likely to use them as they would other public access computers, such as for e-mails or writing papers.

We have encouraged patrons to use the iPads to take photos, share documents, and keep track of retrieved boxes. In one case a patron was uncomfortable replacing photocopies with snapshots from the iPad. This patron was new to archival research, found the iPad distracting from his main objective of researching documents, and instead used his laptop and requested photocopies. However, he later used the iPad to review the finding aid and select additional boxes to use. We have found this kind of experience is common in people who are reluctant to use them at first—eventually we find these people picking up the iPads and finding them helpful after all.

One of the unique and most beneficial aspects of using the iPad camera is working with negatives, which have always been a time-consuming and labor-intensive process. We have a light table for researchers to review negatives, but patrons might not know what they were ordering until they purchased a scan and saw the positive image. We have a large collection of a local newspaper's negatives that are accessed regularly, and the collection is particularly difficult to access because large sets of negatives are stored in envelopes, making it difficult to separate scan orders from the rest of the envelope without accidentally misfiling or losing frames. By utilizing the iPad camera, patrons can take photos of negatives while viewing them on the light table (see figure 8.1). All photos taken with our iPads are automatically synced to the SCA Dropbox account. Using a staff desktop, Jim downloads the files from Drop-box to our servers and makes a copy for our own permanent use and another one for the patron. Using Photoshop, he batch-processes the im-ages by first inverting and then creating a low-resolution positive copy. We then e-mail the low-resolution positives to the patron. While this process may take a few more steps than before, our patrons now order fewer images because they now know what they are getting. In the past, many patrons would order an entire strip of six frames just to use one frame. We explored apps that patrons could use to convert from negative to positive, but with many patrons being new to using iPads in this way, it was quicker and easier for us to convert them.

Of the ten to twelve researchers that have used iPads to photograph negatives, almost all have expressed a positive experience. It particularly helps when patrons are unable to come view the negatives in person, so a staff member takes photos, e-mails them to the patron, and the patron responds with a scan order. One patron who utilized this option in per-

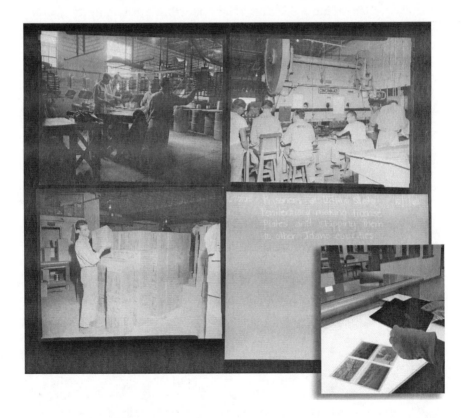

Figure 8.1.   Example of an iPad photo of negatives with identification turned into a positive image; staff taking photo at the light table. *Photo by Jim Duran*

son often only had about thirty to forty-five minutes a week to examine negatives for a large project. By taking photos of the negatives, he quickly assessed them, took pictures, and then did a closer examination after we e-mailed him the positive images. These are low resolution, therefore there is no concern about reproducing without permission. This patron took full advantage of this new service and in about two months ordered eighty-seven scanned images. After finishing the project, he came back to express his appreciation and also suggested that a photo-editing app might make the image selection process easier, which we will investigate.

Although we haven't received a lot of feedback about specific apps, we paid careful attention to our first several patron interactions with the iPads. From those instances we found file sharing and storage to be a very crucial aspect of a patron's needs. We initially started using Google Drive but experienced numerous issues with it. Even if a patron had a Gmail account, it did not always sync correctly, and it involved more steps. We later switched to Dropbox, and indeed at least one patron specifically recommended we stick to Dropbox because he was already familiar with that cloud storage service.

An unexpected challenge was the number of researchers who had never used an iPad or mobile device for library research, including graduate students and local historians. We sometimes spent extra time covering basic instructions on operating the iPad in addition to searching our resources. Though undergraduates are often more familiar with using mobile devices, our diverse patron population sometimes requires further instruction and staff time. However, we see this as an opportunity to educate our patrons while complying with Boise State University's campuswide mobile-learning initiatives.

To help assess our success with using iPads in the reading room, we keep an open dialogue with the users. We continually ask researchers for feedback on how useful the iPad was to their work so we can improve their use. One out-of-state researcher commented that he had not yet seen iPads in reading rooms and found it helpful because he could have the finding aid open on the iPad while making notes on his laptop. We also observed patrons interact with the devices while they researched. So far, the most compliments received are on the benefits of taking photos of negatives. We have not kept formal statistics and will explore whether that is necessary for the future. We measured success by noticing an increased use of the iPads by all patrons, including undergraduates, graduate students, and local and other outside researchers. In addition to the nine participants in the community workshop, they were used in three history classes, with a total of thirty-three students and three faculty, plus two sections of the kinesiology class with about sixty students.

Though the main goal of bringing iPads into SCA was for patrons, we also found them beneficial for internal staff use. One unanticipated use was with exhibit installation. While creating a small three-case exhibit,

Cheryl accessed documents through Dropbox and used her own iPad's notes feature to go back and forth between exhibit layout and items to ensure there were captions for all items. The archivist laid out the exhibit on a large table not near a computer, so the mobile device saved taking notes on paper and instead provided an easy solution to writing item captions, as the notes could be easily copied and pasted into a Word document. Another helpful use was the FaceTime application. With only a four-person staff, historically one person always stays behind to cover the reading room for all library meetings or events. We used iPads so that person can now "attend" staff meetings or other presentations through FaceTime. One staff member takes the iPad, sets it in front of the meeting, and turns on FaceTime, which activates a video conference to the person who remains in the reading room.

LESSONS LEARNED

While overall our experience implementing iPads in the reading room has been relatively painless, we have learned some things during the eight months we've been using them. Some aspects have taken us more time than we anticipated, and others have been simpler than we feared. For example, some staff time is often required to assist patrons in using iPads for their needs, but this is easily incorporated into general explanations of reading room procedures and using archival collections. At the service moment, it adds time, but as more people become familiar with using mobile tablets, we expect this will decrease. There is also potential to save time for staff because we will have fewer photocopy and scan requests to fulfill when patrons take advantage of using the iPad's camera features.

A primary consideration of incorporating iPads into a reading room is security. We valued ease of use over security risks, and because we have a small reading room with four tables visible from the reference desk, it is easy for us to monitor their use. As noted, we have not had any iPads go missing in the time that they have been available. We believed that the functionality we would lose by securing the iPads to tables overruled the potential risk, and so far that risk hasn't backfired.

While we were all comfortable using iPads ourselves because of the university's and library's mobile-learning initiatives, training could be another important aspect for people in other institutions. How familiar are staff with using iPads? Will they need training? Are they comfortable enough with the technology to help patrons learn how to use them? In our case we were already familiar with the technology, so no training was required, and it was simple for us to educate researchers on using the iPads.

Another aspect is managing maintenance and technical issues. Implementing procedures for adding apps initially and in the future and for regular reimaging of the iPads was an ongoing discussion prior to and after we received the iPads. The library IT staff's experience with reimaging the library's circulating and instruction iPads made it an easy transition for us to reimage the iPads to clear browser history, photos, and any saved passwords or cookies. IT was already using Apple Configurator, a free mobile device–management software that can format thirty to sixty mobile devices at once. In less than a minute, we are able to reimage our iPads simply by connecting them to a dedicated laptop.

While we were happy to receive three of our own designated iPads, the ones we received were hand-me-downs. The library did not purchase new iPads for our reading room but instead repurposed unused ones. In the future and as the library budget allows, we hope to update our iPad 1s to iPad 3s (or later versions). The major impediment to the iPad 1 is the lack of a camera, which is an essential component of how our researchers use them. Also, they are being phased out, and the iOS is no longer updated.

We continually look for new apps to include on our reading room iPads. We plan on adding Google Earth so researchers can access our aerial photo index. We also plan on experimenting with displaying georeferenced photographs, and Google Earth will be useful for that project. We will experiment with using a flashlight application as a quick substitute for a light table. Hopefully patrons will be able to set the iPad on the reading room table with the flashlight app activated and use the surface to preview photo negatives. This is an option for when our traditional light table is in use.

The biggest challenge we encountered was finding the best way to transfer images from the iPad to the patron. At first we used Google Drive to sync photos to e-mail accounts because the entire campus uses Google accounts. The use of iPads, however, will not allow multiple users to sign in to Google accounts. To avoid the potential security risks of requiring patrons to use their own accounts, we signed in to Google Drive using our general archives account and then handed the patron the iPad to add pictures using the iPad camera. This was not ideal because patrons would have access to the archives e-mail.

When using the Google Drive app, users can take pictures that save directly to Google's cloud storage. If the patron accidentally started taking pictures using the native camera app, those files could only be saved to the Google Drive one by one. An additional problem with Google Drive was its camera app only presented a quarter-screen preview of the image, making it difficult to take pictures. Another complication that made the process fail was that the Boise State student e-mail accounts are not set up to authenticate in the Google Drive app on an iPad. We ultimately discontinued this application for transferring images due to these irreconcilable issues.

We also experimented with researchers signing into their own e-mail accounts and e-mailing all photos to themselves, but this proved to be an issue for researchers who took a large quantity of photos as well as a security problem if they did not sign out. Additionally, it prohibited us from tracking how many images were taken during the research process.

The solution we ultimately implemented was to create a Dropbox account with our general archives e-mail (archives@boisestate.edu). It is set it up so that every photo taken with the patron iPads automatically syncs to the same "Camera Uploads" Dropbox folder, streamlining the process and not adding any steps for the patron or us to transfer from the iPad. We then access the Dropbox folder from a computer to either e-mail them to the patron (if a small number) or share a folder with their photos, so he or she can easily download the images. This option proved to be effective, straightforward, and easy, however it will require us to develop a content-management policy for our Dropbox account. For example, we will need to decide on a time limit for shared folders and a naming schema.

Although we are happy with our Dropbox solution, we also tested the connectivity of new apps to e-mail and cloud storage and found some of the third-party camera apps added additional steps for syncing pictures to file-sharing options. One camera app in particular did not have an easy way to file share but had other features for adding text, shapes, and lines to photos. We decided to stick with the Apple camera app even though it lacked some additional features because it seamlessly synced with most file-sharing platforms, including Dropbox. Seamless connectivity was crucial for our use of the iPads because additional file-sharing steps could confuse our patrons and add to staff workflow.

Having options for file sharing is crucial when using mobile devices. While we were not able to successfully use Google Drive to share files with patrons for this project, the process of learning and implementing it was beneficial. Having the ability to offer patrons multiple options for sharing their digital files can significantly improve satisfaction with researchers. We will continue to monitor options in addition to Dropbox that can better serve our patrons.

CONCLUSION

Overall, we achieved great success in integrating iPad use into the reading room and other SCA activities. We cannot imagine not having them and continually discuss other potential uses and options to create better service to our patrons.

One of our next steps is to make sure we have four iPads permanently in the reading room, preferably iPad 2s or later so that they have cameras. Having one per table appears sufficient for our current needs, though we may explore having more in the future. We will continue to ask patrons about apps or other resources that would be helpful in using iPads for their research. We also reviewed the article "Apps for Archivists" in the September/October 2012 *Archival Outlook* and followed up to find out more information about the "Technology Petting Zoo" at ACRL's Rare Books and Manuscripts Section (RBMS) annual meeting.

We will also explore how to further integrate iPad use in archives instruction. There is currently a master of applied historical research graduate program that focuses on technology and public history, and other programs continue to incorporate technology and mobile learning into their curricula. By working with the faculty and students in this program, we learn about developments in the public history field that may benefit us. Additionally, we can have students evaluate our resources and provide feedback for improvement. This type of collaboration strengthens our relationship with departments while giving everyone more ideas on use and implementation of mobile technology.

We have found making iPads available in the reading room to be a great benefit to providing access to archives resources. It helps us stay current on larger technology trends as well as demonstrates to patrons that we seek to adapt to their needs. Working with faculty and students who use our materials for projects can help us further our goals of increasing use of our collections while simultaneously helping us understand our researchers' needs.

The success of this initial experiment is largely due to the time we spent investigating how to make the iPads in the reading room work for patrons, as well as the support of the library administration. A rewarding part of this project was to witness the excitement of patrons as they used iPads and realized how they were beneficial to their research. This project is hopefully the first of many ways we will explore bringing archives resources to patrons using mobile technology.

Cheryl Oestreicher is head of special collections and archives and assistant professor; Julia Stringfellow is archivist, librarian, and assistant professor; and Jim Duran is archives associate at Boise State University.

NOTES

1. Task Force for Teaching, Learning, and Technology, "Mobile-Learning for Boise State: A Proposal to Catalyze a Transformation in Teaching and Learning," *Boise State University*, Fall 2011, http://mobilelearning.boisestate.edu/images/MobileLearningProposal_Oct.pdf.

2. See the "Access to Research Materials" section in Society of American Archivists, *Best Practices for Working with Archives Researchers with Physical Disabilities*, June 2010, accessed August 22, 2013, www2.archivists.org/sites/all/files/BestPract-Disabilities_Researchers_0.pdf.

NINE

Beyond "Trial by Fire"

*Toward a More Active Approach to Training New
Reference Staff*

Marc Brodsky, Virginia Tech

All of us who do reference work began without knowing much about our collections and with an incomplete knowledge, at best, of the tools at hand with which we now do our jobs. Over time we have undergone a process of on-the-job training, with the result that we have gotten better, even become good or expert, at providing reference services to our patrons. It is a process that consists of a blend of self-education, practice, and assistance from others, along with ever-increasing experience. An important part of most reference archivists' jobs is to help others on this journey by training new staff members in the collections and idiosyncrasies of their particular repositories. As the staff at special collections at Virginia Tech has grown in recent months, this question of training new staff in the specifics of doing reference at our collection has become a matter of some interest. How would this best be accomplished? How could we help to produce efficient, knowledgeable, and effective professionals who can help connect patrons with the materials they seek, often without, of course, the patrons knowing exactly what they need?

My own experiences with being trained to work a reference desk as a graduate student worker, intern, and at my first professional job consisted largely of what I have come to call the "discovery method." After an introduction to the materials available, a very brief orientation to the tools at my disposal, and some time to acquaint myself with those tools, I was put on the desk—not completely alone at first but nearly so. Soon

123

after that I was on my own. Speaking informally with colleagues, I have found that this method, in which success depends on passing through a kind of "trial by fire," is not at all uncommon.

As I recalled my own earlier experiences and imagined myself in the position of my new coworkers, I was reminded that, even with the training afforded by a degree in library science, one quickly discovers that all online catalogs are not created equal. In archives and special collections, there are often unusual or legacy sources of information that are not readily recognized and finding aids for some collections but not all. As the types of materials vary, so might the tools, lists, and databases used to discover or provide access to them. It can be a confusing scenario for any new archivist, as it surely was for me when I first started. I was lucky to have had a couple of colleagues who had been there for some time, so I had the benefit of their institutional memories and experiences. I asked them lots of questions, as I was urged to do. But now I began to consider whether and how those institutional memories, now including mine, might be put to better use in helping my new colleagues. I also, more abstractly, considered the need for a strategy if the appearance of new staff coincided with the departure of more experienced members of the staff—through retirement or any other situation—and important sources of institutional memories were not available. How then to assist with the transfer of knowledge to new people whose job it had become to field incoming inquiries?

PLANNING

I had not really thought much about the process of educating a reference archivist since my own "initiation" into the practice. To be clear, my subject here is not the education of those training to become archivists, whether at school, in certification programs, or even in a variety of internships or other apprentice-like situations that are part of most archival education programs. There is a large, varied, and active literature on these matters. In 1977, Frank B. Evans could write an article titled "Post-appointment Archival Training: A Proposed Solution for a Basic Problem,"[1] but his subject is embedded in a context in which "preappointment" training, to the extent that there was such a thing, was not yet grounded in archival methodology, as it is at today's professional library and information science graduate programs. Twenty years later, in 1997, Terry Eastwood suggests a model for a course on public services, with the goal of creating a "service ethos" lacking among archivists.[2] Here again Eastwood, in pointing out a deficiency among practicing archivists, identifies an element missing from their training in programs of archival education. For today's archivist, our own user-centered universe suggests that the transition to a public service model has been, largely, successfully negotiated.

But some of the literature, engaged as it often is in the debates and specifics of what should constitute a proper form of professional archival training, does offer a possible window on what may be required of the working archivist to become proficient at the job. Although I conducted a literature review only as preparation for this article, I did find it interesting to see how characteristics of the successful reference archivist have previously been described. One key and uncontroversial element is the accumulation of knowledge—regarding the contents of one's repository and more general subject-based knowledge—often expressed as a function of time. When addressing inadequate service due, for example, to an archivist's inexperience and limited knowledge of the archives, Stuart Strachan writes, "it can take up to five or six years of fairly intensive experience for an archivist to become reasonably familiar with the full range of resources in a large repository."[3] Similarly, Le Roy Barnett offers the following advice:

> Unfortunately, there are no secrets or shortcuts to a skill level in any field. In order to obtain a high degree of competency, one must devote years of professional and personal time to studying the subject(s) for which you are responsible. Consequently, I seriously doubt if any good reference person confines their job-enhancing activities to just weekday hours between 8:00 a.m. and 5:00 p.m. To do the task well almost certainly requires a lifetime of business and private commitment to the cause.[4]

Both Strachan and Barnett, writing in 1996 and 1997, respectively, have suggestions on how to close the gap. Barnett, long-time reference archivist at the State Archives of Michigan at the time, says "to be a good reference person is to fully expose yourself in the subject area(s) for which you are responsible." Under the heading of "self-improvement," he describes reading or becoming very familiar with every major work about Michigan. If a topic of repeated inquiry was not adequately covered in the literature, he often conducted original research and published on the matter. He spent breaks examining "every book in a particular section of the library" and suggests reading finding aids during short moments of free time.[5] Strachan emphasizes the importance of substance over process and suggests training in "nineteenth-century official publications, provincial government archives, administrative history or the land system, twentieth-century politicians' papers, and so on" rather than in "spreadsheets, time management, or transparency" for new archivists.[6]

Nobody would dispute that increasing one's knowledge of the subjects represented in one's repository will produce a better reference archivist, but I would no more suggest to a newly hired colleague at the reference desk to accept as a long-range goal, for example, the reading of every book about the Civil War in Virginia than I would pass along Barnett's extolling the virtues of using a telephone with a long cord while speaking with patrons. This is not because knowing more about Virginia history during the war won't be helpful to me or my colleague on the job, but at a time when information is so much more easily and quickly available than it was in the mid-1990s, the points of emphasis and perspectives on how to develop as a reference archivist are necessarily different from what they were twenty years ago. Certainly, purely factual and basic information about subjects and topics is often easily available via the web.

With regard to the content of collections, the development of searchable databases, while not replacing the need to know the materials on the shelves and in the boxes, can make it easier to find appropriate materials for a patron even if an archivist has little or no explicit knowledge of those materials. But there will always be those materials that are not discoverable online or via databases or other search venues because the level of available description is sparse. The contents of vertical files, for example, or materials held in institutional record groups that are only described at a series or collection level may be overlooked if searching catalogues or databases of finding aids is presumed to produce a sufficient reply to every inquiry. If information about these uncataloged or undercataloged sources is not accessible via online or other tools, then a dependence on those tools alone will often produce an insufficient response. Use of these tools may produce an initial and successful result that points the way to useful materials for a patron, but it may not be a complete response. Going beyond this initial stage—or, more properly, not going beyond this first stage—is often when new or inexperienced archivists encounter trouble. Today, while it would be wonderful to know something about every major book or piece in the collection about Virginia, to effectively provide reference services, it is more important that I and my colleagues know when we have completed a search for materials on a given topic and, more importantly, when that search has not yet been reasonably finished. Though perhaps a subtle shift in emphasis, this does represent for the reference archivist a change in the way the job has historically been approached and accomplished.

What then is to be done? How should I plan to help and encourage the transfer of knowledge to my new colleagues to assist them with their reference duties? In *Providing Reference Services for Archives and Manuscripts*, Mary Jo Pugh tells us, "Staff development programs to train junior staff and to ensure continuity of reference services and subject expertise are important,"[7] yet no discussion of the details of such programs follows. Perhaps the nature of such programs is clear to everyone, but have details been offered, explained, or discussed? Is there recognition among reference professionals that it may be inadequate to put new staff on the desk after some short period of reviewing the appropriate tools—online and otherwise—and let them fend for themselves, even with the admonition to ask questions when necessary? The potential impact on patrons is that they receive less-than-ideal service, which may then in turn leave them with an unsatisfactory opinion of the repository. Or they may leave satisfied but without knowing about important resources in the collection that might have also helped them. For new staffers it puts them in an untenable position in which they are being asked to succeed but without having received the preparation required to ensure that success. Is this the best we can do to serve the public and support our colleagues?

All too often the assumption seems to be that if we hire smart, capable people, over time and as the need arises, they will discover what they need to know. While I agree that "learning by doing" is certainly an important component of the process, I wanted to explore how that part of the process could be actively augmented to make it more effective and efficient. Looking back on my own early experiences, it was several months after I began working reference before I asked the right coworker the appropriate question that led to my being told about a card file that contained information about students at the university during its first few decades—a resource that in retrospect seems crucial to someone working in a university archives! What could I do to make sure my new colleagues received a better introduction than I did?

I think the key element to creating a better training experience is to create *intentional* learning experiences, as contrasted with the largely accidental ones of the "discovery method" I and others experienced. The notion of preparation must be taken seriously in the planning of any such process. The best preparation and perhaps the most important overall element is to create the greatest number of opportunities for engagement with the widest range of materials in the collection. This assumes a situation in which all of the reference staff are responsible for working with the entire range of collections. Where a more strict division of responsibility is in place, staff might be asked to specialize more directly in a given area. Still, the creation of opportunities to engage—thoughtfully, actively, and beyond the reference desk—with collections and materials is an essential starting point.

Another important element in creating a productive training environment is patience. This on-the-job education will take time, and an expectation and understanding that this is the case should be built into the process for all concerned. It is fair to say that, even after five years, I am certainly still learning about our collections and sometimes need to be reminded about certain infrequently used tools and materials that might be exactly what is needed in response to a particular inquiry. For a new reference archivist, the immediate goal is to attain as quickly as possible a level of expertise equal to the task of assisting patrons. Despite the urgency often felt by those new to the job, they should be patient enough to grant themselves permission to take extra time with materials whenever possible. The benefit of just spending time in the rare books shelves or perusing the contents of a folder of photographs after retrieving images for a patron cannot be emphasized enough. Although experienced hands should recognize this practice as an essential way to prepare for future inquiries, newer archivists may not or may even be concerned that other staff won't regard this time as well spent.

For those other staff members, patience may mean, for example, recognizing that need for new staff to take the time to explore materials. It also means cultivating a willingness to share inquiries, results, and replies with a new colleague, even if she or he doesn't ask. (Although new staff members are often urged to ask as many questions as possible, for many reasons some may not ask often enough.) Patience on the part of experienced staff may also be needed when answering the same question from a new coworker several times. Again, often the only way to learn is to ask, and sometimes a wealth of new information can be confusing. There is also a lot to remember. Those who have been at the collection for some time may find it hard to remember what it was like when they were new, but they still need to be willing to patiently put aside other tasks in the interest of helping the new folks. This needn't take a lot of time, and the result will be well worth the effort.

Last (and always), there is practice, something that can take many forms. A greater number of hours on the desk, for example, may be preferable to fewer. Instead of continuing to distribute incoming electronic inquiries among experienced staff in the same manner as before the arrival of new staff, inquiries may be increasingly directed toward the newer people. Questions that arrive from off site and that may either require or simply be allowed more time could be shared by both an inexperienced and more experienced archivist. Or the latter could review the reference process and result before a reply is sent to the patron. Also, we should not underestimate the value of opportunities to gain reference experience without the patron standing nearby expecting perfectly appropriate materials to spring from each tap, tap, tap on a keyboard. In this regard there also is nothing wrong with posing real questions but with no actual patron asking. Recently received—and completed—inquiries can provide a useful and interesting experience when posed as practice. Anxiety needn't always accompany a new person's effort to respond to a question!

IMPLEMENTATION

At this point it is important to say that this "program" was not devised or even imagined prior to our hiring of new staff—three new people in six months—whose duties would include weekly hours on the reference desk. For this first influx of new people since I started working at special collections, there was no deliberate development of a plan for their training beyond the usual "discovery method." There were no procedures put in place to review, modify, or assess their progress. Rather, after new staff members had come on board, received the usual minimal training, and were let loose on the reference desk, a series of observations over the course of a few months led me to consider the inadequacy of the usual method and both the need for and shape of a remedy.

Too often after an initial search turned up some useful material in response to a reference question, new staff members were not making subsequent efforts to find additional material. Whether they were too easily satisfied or just relieved to find something relevant is unclear, but appropriate materials, fairly obvious to those of us on staff with more experience, were not always being brought to patrons. To me it was clear that this was not a problem with our new people but was attributable to the inadequate training they received. Only recently and after an admittedly piecemeal approach have the components of a plan dedicated to improvement in reference training begun to take shape. Although this perhaps is not an ideal process, change often occurs in this way, and we will be in a much better position the next time new folks arrive.

There were, however, several duties assigned to our new coworkers that clearly helped to develop the engagement with collections that is an essential part of preparing oneself to do reference work and so can serve as examples of nonreference functions that can be incorporated into reference training. The work contributing to the departmental blog (vtspecial-collections.wordpress.com) and producing exhibits for the department, though not designed as a grounding for reference work, proved to be helpful in unforeseen and indirect ways. In each case it quickly required enough of a familiarity with some aspect of the collection to allow a choice of a topic (presumably among others researched sufficiently to be considered), a selection of materials to highlight, and an opportunity to write in an engaging way about that choice and selection. There is more than one way to build knowledge about materials and collections, and these avenues encourage creativity and can be fun. They get new staff involved in promoting the profile of the department, let their work be seen by the public (who may be or become users of our reference services), and—little by little—help to build a base of expertise. These tasks are also accomplished without the pressure of a waiting patron. In future situations I will be including this work in any new reference training package.

The assignment of special projects—responsibility for a more in-depth engagement with an area or, perhaps, a large collection that needs additional processing (assuming your repository allows overlap of processing and reference responsibilities)—is another indirect method of fostering familiarity with collection materials. More than a blog post or small exhibit, this kind of work builds specific expertise in an area and can, given the concentrated focus and effort, make a colleague the new go-to person for questions in that area or about that collection. This kind of involvement can also, if the fit is particularly good, initiate a lasting interest that will develop over a long period of time. For example, when Virginia Tech's Corps of Cadets faced the challenge of inventorying, boxing, and moving their own historical materials to a "long-term temporary" site in the library with help from special collections, one such opportunity was created for a new coworker. Even though these materials did not belong to special collections, they are mirrored by many materials in our collection that are the subject of many commonly received questions. The project has led not only to a solid accomplishment—important to any new staff member—but also to a desire to build on the experience by learning more about the corps. When I saw my new colleague reading from a multivolume history of the corps at a rare moment of free time at the end of a day, I thought it might not be too long before she becomes the person to whom I go to double- or quickly check a question about the corps that I'm trying to answer.

As important as these indirect preparations are, it is the active and direct support for doing reference work that offers the greatest benefit. In this regard we have recently started having a regular meeting, a voluntary "seminar," occurring every few weeks at which anyone attending can bring a question, raise a matter for discussion, or offer to lead a discussion on a topic. All of us are encouraged to keep a log of received reference questions, noting especially those found to be problematic or difficult, for whatever reason, so that we might review them as a group, perhaps work them as practice, and benefit from our combined experience. Because university archives questions are common, for example, an early matter for our discussion has been the structure and peculiarities of the notebook in which the archives' record groups and subgroups are listed. One suggestion has been to compile a list or wiki of common projects—often relating to matters of local interest or university buildings—that bring students to us semester after semester and that everyone who works the desk is likely to encounter. These first meetings have each concluded with an open discussion of tips and suggestions from those of us who have worked at special collections for a while. The meeting gives us a chance to share bits of accumulated knowledge, not only about materials, but also mini-strategies, such as taking extra time in the rare book room or with the photograph collection that will help someone prepare for the job. You can bet that folks have already been reminded of the card file of early students that remained unknown to me over my first several months!

Just as direct but less structured are the one-on-one conversations that result from an awareness among the staff that, by adding to the knowledge base of our new colleagues and helping them to gain expertise more quickly, we are improving the level of service we provide for our patrons. In other words, *all* of us are now more likely to ask our less-experienced colleagues how their reference work has been going than we were prior to the realization that our standard training was lacking. Those of us working in or near the front desk try to be more aware of incoming patrons when a newer person is at the desk, listening to see if we might be of assistance, just as we are more aware and ready to help when our newer reference staffer goes back to the materials in response to a request. At that point we may very well ask about the specifics of the inquiry, offer to help, or suggest some appropriate material. Given the fine line that can exist between offered assistance and perceived interference, some care may be called for in these instances, but in an established context of mutual support, an offer to help is usually going to be recognized as a positive gesture.

The most structured element in this effort to improve reference training—one we have not yet chosen to pursue—is the creation of a reference manual. These are relatively common tools that can serve a variety of purposes. In *Providing Reference Services*, Pugh offers an appendix of suggested contents for a manual of reference procedures that ranges from administration and finding aids to public programs and security, a wide scope of topics well beyond the issue of responding to reference questions.[8] Especially for this latter purpose, however, expectations that use of a reference manual will solve the problem of inadequate training may need to be tempered. With no hope of being comprehensive—that is, describing all avenues from all types of inquiries—such a manual might potentially become a liability as a crutch that is necessarily incomplete or simply superfluous and sooner or later ignored. At its best, however, perhaps with those most common requests and their recommended sources and avenues of response at its core, a manual would serve as a useful and handy reference to be used when needed. (Indeed, Pugh's list of suggested contents does include "protocols for common questions" among its nearly one hundred suggestions.)

A list of tips that those of us with some experience at special collections take for granted would certainly be an appropriate part of such a manual. For example, when I look at a finding aid and see that the collection's extent is listed as 0.1 cubic feet, I know it's a one-folder collection and I don't need to look up its location because they are all kept in one place. This may be obvious to anyone who has been at special collections for a while but not so clear to those who haven't had the time to make that discovery themselves. This part of the manual could and perhaps should largely be written by the new staff as they either discover or are told some such tip, as they would recognize its significance, whereas more experienced hands tend not to think about them. As procedures and policies change over time, the manual would need to be updated. But it could provide a stable and reliable source of knowledge regarding reference matters for all. Most importantly, perhaps, a written manual would make available to future staffers an institutional memory that can, after all, disappear at any time.

RESULTS

It is too early to assess the results of these efforts in terms of improved performance and training. At this point the only result that can be identified is the enthusiasm with which these efforts have been met by my newer colleagues. Each has greeted the decision to provide more specific training positively and each, while already having "learned the ropes," believes that this new focus on reference training is helping them assist patrons more completely. My more-experienced colleagues have also shown an interest: some perhaps inspired by their own memories of uncomfortable reference situations early in their careers and others simply out of a desire to assist their colleagues. No one, so far, has had a negative comment. The only real difficulty has been trying to schedule a time when all of us are available to meet and talk.

LESSONS LEARNED

Despite having few firm results at this early stage of our efforts, we have been able to either learn or remind ourselves of some important aspects of reference training. First, it is worth asking if your current process is giving new employees the best possible preparation to help researchers. As I've described, over the past few months at Virginia Tech, we decided that our standard method of simply "learning by doing" was not acceptable. Too often it has left our people both unprepared and, perhaps, uncomfortable in their handling of patron's questions. It is not that this method takes too long; rather we believe it just takes longer than it needs to. If we can put our mutual experience to work for our newer colleagues, the result will be an improvement in effectiveness and efficiency. Patrons will get better responses, and we hope our new staff will feel less stress and more satisfaction in the job they are doing. They will also have more concrete evidence that we, as an institution, value reference work because we think it important enough to direct more time and effort in this training.

In my own case, I have been reminded that not everyone will ask questions, even if urged to do so. Some people will not say "yes" when asked in the middle of a search if they could use a hand. The reason for the regular meeting to discuss sources and methods and questions and responses is to create a space in which asking questions and sharing knowledge is precisely the purpose of the meeting. Knowing that other people need to ask questions, are asking questions, have asked questions, regardless of how long they've worked reference, can sometimes be all that is required to make staffers easier about admitting that they didn't yet know what they haven't had time to learn. It is a situation all of us understand. Also, if we do compile a reference manual, as I think we will, we will measurably add to the resources available to those who will provide reference services in the future and offer another avenue for them to learn the tricks and the trade.

CONCLUSION

To continue to do something as it has always been done simply because it has always been done that way is bad practice. Setting a new reference staffer loose to "discover" the route to excellent reference service may be the way it has always been done but may not be the best way to reach the desired goal. At Virginia Tech we concluded that this method wasn't working well enough and probably never really did. We decided that a more active and intentional approach could produce a tangible benefit.

The essential element in making such an approach work effectively, as is the case with all projects that involve more than one person, is not only a willingness to communicate but also a requirement, if not an enthusiasm, for communication. The tangible benefit from an effort that is about sharing knowledge only becomes possible if everyone is committed to a free and ready flow of information. Although this simple truth is obvious, it is not unknown for an institution's work culture to make such an effort difficult. However, once any obstacles are acknowledged and this commitment is secured, then the next matter is to choose the method of the communication—and there are many choices. Again, the obvious choice is to employ the methods that the individuals involved will use. Earlier, I mentioned maintaining a wiki of common projects that bring students into the repository. This could also be used for building the list of tips that might be part of a reference manual. Such a manual, with all of its diverse content, including policies, procedures, and methods, might itself exist as this kind of shared online document. If people were hesitant about creating a wiki, perhaps a series of shared GoogleDocs would work as well. Or, working hand in hand, the latter could provide the staging, the informal site for thoughts and concerns that, once agreed to, would become part of the documentation at the wiki. If a physical notebook was preferred, that, too, might be produced. The format of the final product is not nearly as important as the commitment to produce and use that product.

Another possible model for sharing information, and one that might work better for people who are more comfortable with visual learning, could be a video tour of the repository. This strategy could be used in situations where a particularly experienced archivist or perhaps a lone arranger is leaving an institution. Based on the more common model of a video tour of the public side of the archives intended for users, this tour would review the areas and materials behind the scenes. These videos might remind a new archivist of some collection of materials or a newspaper collection perhaps, show its location, and offer recorded commentary from more experienced coworkers. Another video might demonstrate procedures, for example, for how to fulfill an image request from a patron; the video would include such information as the location of forms, questions to ask, and common problems. For the reference desk itself, an app like Twitsper (an amalgam of *Twitter* and *whisper* that allows for tweets to be sent only to a select list of recipients—perhaps particularly appropriate for a reading room where quiet is usually maintained) might allow a staffer's request for assistance to go out in real time to other members of the reference staff. Though not appropriate for all repositories due to physical configuration and the close proximity of coworkers, a tool like this might be useful for some. Again, the best array of methods for sharing knowledge will be determined by the usefulness of those methods as defined by the people involved. No one method is likely to be adequate for any single location; none will be right for all.

There is also a need for further discussion within the profession about programs and methods such as those mentioned here. The sharing of lessons learned and new ideas will help pave the way for newly arrived archivists to succeed more readily at providing good reference service. Within any given repository, one should also not forget to involve management, as appropriate, to help gain support and acceptance of these programs.

At Virginia Tech we have just started down this road. After recognizing a problem, we are determined to create a better path. Along the way, not only do we expect to produce archivists more expert at reference, but also we hope to gain better relationships among an already collegial staff that does however sometimes tend to work too much in isolation from each other. We think a more seamless, quicker, and richer integration of new staff members into the workflow and culture of special collections is a worthwhile goal and a fully achievable result. In the end, of course, success means consistently providing the most expert reference services to our patrons. This is the goal all service-oriented archivists seek and is the result that all of our training, knowledge, and experience is meant to achieve.

Marc Brodsky *is public services and reference archivist, special collections at the University Libraries, Virginia Tech.*

NOTES

1. Frank B. Evans, "Postappointment Archival Training: A Proposed Solution for a Basic Problem," *The American Archivist* 40, no. 1 (1977), 57–74.

2. Terry Eastwood, "Public Services Education for Archivists," in *Reference Services for Archives & Manuscripts*, ed. Laura B. Cohen (New York: Haworth Press, 1997), 27–38.

3. Stuart Strachan, "How Good Are We? Sketching the Parameters of Service Evaluation," *Archifacts* (April 1996), 52.

4. Le Roy Barnett, "Sitting in the Hot Seat: Some Thoughts from the Reference Chair," in *Reference Services for Archives and Manuscripts*, ed. Laura B. Cohen (New York: Haworth Press, 1997), 44.

5. Ibid., 42–44.

6. Strachan, 52–53.

7. Mary Jo Pugh, *Providing Reference Services for Archives & Manuscripts* (Chicago: Society of American Archivists, 2005), 250.

8. Pugh, 323–27.

TEN

Access for All

Making Your Archives' Website Accessible for People with Disabilities

Lisa Snider

In 1997 Tim Berners-Lee, the inventor of the World Wide Web, wrote, "The power of the web is in its universality. Access by everyone regardless of disability is an essential aspect."[1] However, more than sixteen years later, users with disabilities are not always able to gain full access to web content. This is unacceptable, considering that, according to the World Health Organization, there are an estimated one billion people worldwide, or 15 percent of the world's population, who live with a disability.[2] In the United States alone, out of 291.1 million people, 54.4 million (18.7 percent) identified as having some level of disability, and among this population, 34.9 million (12 percent) identified as having a severe disability.[3] How does this translate to archives? If an archives' website gets 1,000 visitors every year, then it is possible that at least 150 of them identify as having some sort of disability. That is a lot of visitors!

I first got involved with website accessibility and usability issues in 1999 when I started a web development business. Over the past fourteen years, I have continually educated myself on website accessibility and usability issues, talked with people with disabilities and organizations that supported them, and presented many seminars on the topic. In 2009, I transitioned into a career in archives and started to work with these issues in the archival realm.

However, my passion for ensuring universally accessible websites combined with my new profession fully when I happened upon a meeting of the SAA Accessibility Working Group (AWG) at the 2010 SAA annual conference. The energy and passion for change in the room was electric, and I was inspired by the commitment of the co-coordinators, Daria D'Arienzo and Debra Kimok. The AWG members had been focusing on physical accessibility and had provided excellent resources for archivists.[4] I joined the group right away and focused on website accessibility. Since then, I have given many presentations on website accessibility and usability at archival association conferences, conducted a research study on the accessibility and usability of Canadian archival websites, and am now focused on the topic of universal accessibility and digital preservation.

Every time I give a website accessibility and usability presentation to archivists, I always get asked such questions as "Where can I start?" and "Can I get tips for my IT staff, my manager, and myself?" This article is focused on answering these questions as well as providing an overview of the basics of universally accessible websites for archivists. It will be useful whether you have a very basic website or one that includes a catalogue or search function, digitized or born-digital images or photographs, digitized manuscripts, or text documents.

BACKGROUND ISSUES

Terminology

Terminology is always changing in the disability field. While some people or organizations may use one phrase or term, others may not be in agreement. Additionally, different phrases or terms may be used at different times or in different parts of the world. In North America, it is generally agreed that the terms *handicapped* and *crippled* should not be used, and the word *impairment* may be problematic. For example, the National Association of the Deaf prefers the terms *deaf, deafened*, or *hard of hearing* over the phrase *hearing impaired* because they feel those terms are more positive and don't imply a deficit.[5]

The term *disability* can also be problematic. Many advocates and organizations do not use it because it becomes a measure against ability, which can imply "being less than." Whenever possible, I prefer to use more-inclusive phrases, such as *people with different abilities* or *differently abled people*, because they put the person first. I also prefer the phrase *universally accessible website* over *accessible website*. For me, a universally accessible website is accessible for all viewers regardless of ability.

We can't always know what term or phrase a particular person or organization may prefer, so just do your best. If you are unsure about terminology or any other issue, don't be afraid to ask the differently abled patron or employee you are working with for guidance, or contact a local disability-related organization for help.

Making the Case for Universal Accessibility

When I talk with other archivists about universally accessible websites, they all agree that it is an important issue. However, in many cases we have to prove to our administrators that the time and money needed to make websites universally accessible is justified. For this purpose I developed a list of seven major benefits of making archives' websites universally accessible.

Universal Accessibility Meets Our Ethical Code

In North America archivists are guided by our national associations' codes of ethics, and they mandate equitable access for patrons. For example, in the SAA *Code of Ethics for Archivists*, there is an "Access and Use" provision that reads in part, "Archivists actively promote open and equitable access to the records in their care. . . . They minimize restrictions and maximize ease of access. They facilitate the continuing accessibility and intelligibility of archival materials in all formats."[6]

Universal Accessibility Increases Usability for All Patrons

A universally accessible website benefits many users, not just differently abled ones. These include older people, those with low literacy skills, those using such technologies or devices as smartphones and tablets, and users who do not have access to high-speed Internet.

Why is this so? When we make a website more accessible, we have to look carefully at how the content, navigation, and layout is being presented and used. This benefits everyone. In addition, a universally accessible website should use standardized HTML and Cascading Style Sheet (CSS) code. This can make the layout and design more usable overall because it lessens issues with different devices or computers that are used to view the site.

Universal Accessibility Increases Visibility

In my experience universally accessible websites are more likely to come up in search engine results and be given a higher ranking in them. The higher rank could be due to proper search engine optimization. However, it can also be due to the universally accessible code and content on the page, as this makes it easier and quicker for search engine spiders to crawl through your webpages. If you make it easier for the spiders or crawlers, they may reward you with increased coverage, or higher rankings! Increased coverage may bring you more patrons and help raise your profile in the local community and the world.

Universal Accessibility Means Better-Preserved Websites

Universally accessible websites, in both code and page content, are more likely to "[facilitate] better website archiving and replay."[7] Many archivists are preserving websites with such software as Archive-It, which is based on the Heritrix web crawler. As a result they are seeing what web developers already knew: The better sites are constructed (in terms of universally accessible code and content), the easier it is for the crawler to read them, and thus they are more fully and accurately preserved. Preservation web crawlers, such as Heritrix, access websites like a search engine spider or crawler.[8] If we make it easy for the crawler to do its job, then we will be rewarded with better-preserved websites. This means that our own archives' sites will be better preserved, and we can help our parent organizations and donors make sure their websites are also properly preserved for future generations.

Universal Accessibility Saves Time and Money

Many archives' budgets are shrinking, and websites are increasingly being used to help the public with their basic inquiries. If we make our websites universally accessible, we could help lower the number of basic inquiries received through phone, e-mail, or in-person visits.

Universal Accessibility Avoids Potential Legal Action

Universal accessibility can help organizations avoid potential lawsuits. There have been two recent accessibility lawsuits related to library websites. One was a complaint filed in 2010 by the National Federation of the Blind against Penn State University.[9] It stated that the library's website was not fully accessible to students who are blind and that this violated their civil rights under the Americans with Disabilities Act (ADA). This lawsuit was settled, but it sent shockwaves through the American university system. As a result, many universities, such as the University of Iowa, started to improve the universal accessibility of their websites.[10] Additionally, in September 2012, a student who is blind filed a similar complaint against the University of Montana.[11] He could not access course materials that included digitized images on webpages, noncaptioned videos, and inaccessible library database materials. While these suits were not brought against archives, this kind of litigation could easily move into the archival realm.

Universal Accessibility Meets Potential Legislative Mandates

Universally accessible websites allow an archives to comply with accessibility-related policies or antidiscrimination legislation in their work environment or country. The complaint against Penn State noted earlier was based on violations of the ADA. While this act does not currently cover websites, many lawsuits against inaccessible websites have been successfully pursued under it.[12] Amendments to the act to specifically include websites are expected to be ratified very soon.[13]

The second piece of American legislation to be aware of is section 508 of the Rehabilitation Act of 1973 (as amended in 1998). This requires that electronic and information technology, such as websites, which are developed, procured, maintained, or used by federal departments or agencies, be made accessible. Section 508 includes sixteen technical standards specifically for website accessibility. Although this act is geared toward U.S. federal agencies or departments, many businesses and organizations worldwide use these standards for their websites.

In contrast, Canada does not have federal accessibility-related legislation. It does have the Human Rights Act and the Canadian Charter of Rights and Freedoms. While these don't specifically mention websites, a successful lawsuit has taken place based on the charter.[14] Provincial accessibility acts do exist. The province of Manitoba recently introduced their provincial accessibility act.[15] Quebec has also enacted its own act, which includes government websites.[16] As well, the province of Ontario has the Accessibility for Ontarians with Disabilities Act, which was recently updated to include government, designated–public sector, and large organization websites.[17]

Types of Disabilities and Related Assistive Devices and Technologies

The patrons who come to your website may identify as having a specific type of disability or multiple disabilities, and they may be using different assistive devices or technologies to view your content. The following are the four types of disabilities and their associated technologies that you should focus on when building universally accessible websites.

Visual Disabilities: Blindness, Low Vision, Color Blindness, and So On

People who are blind or have no functional vision will likely use screen-reader software on their computers or devices to navigate and read webpages. This software converts what it navigates and reads into a voice synthesizer or refreshable Braille display. These patrons don't usually use a mouse but instead use the keyboard to navigate the screen reader through a site. Site visitors with some functional vision or low vision may use screen-magnification software, which allows the screen content to be enlarged by at least 100 to 200 percent. Others will manually increase the size of the text or change the color contrast in their Internet browsers.

Viewers who are color blind can't always see the contrast between certain colors used on your website. The most common is the red/green color combination and in rare cases the blue/yellow color combination. No studies have been found that show how these viewers counteract this issue.

Auditory Disabilities: Deafness, Hardness of Hearing, and So On

People who are deaf or deafened (later in life) don't usually use special devices to view webpages. Some people can use hearing aids, but it depends on the severity of their deafness. Those who can't hear audio or video materials may try to read lips (if appropriate), read text captions or transcripts, or need a sign language interpreter. Many people who are deaf learned sign language as their first language, so if it is not made available, it may present a barrier. A patron who is hard of hearing may either use a hearing aid or a software or hardware sound amplifier to hear audio or video materials.

Physical Disabilities: Partial or Total Loss of Limb Function or Dexterity

There are many different kinds of motor and dexterity impairments that can lead to partial or total loss of function in a limb or limbs. A patron may have limited or no use of their arms or hands, or they may be missing one or both of their arms or hands. Many of these viewers can't use a mouse, and instead they may use the keyboard, mouth stick, sip-and-puff switches, joystick, head pointer, or voice system.

Cognitive and Neurological Disabilities: Dyslexia, Attention Deficit Disorder (ADD), Attention Deficit Hyperactivity Disorder (ADHD), Seizure Disorders, and Intellectual or Mental Health Impairments

There are a wide range of cognitive and neurological disabilities, and the severity of them varies greatly. These patrons may use special software. For example, people with dyslexia may use a screen reader or screen-magnification software. Other patrons may not use any special software or hardware. Instead, they may need more time to look at and understand a webpage, or they need a quiet room in order to focus on it. Some people may use speech-enabled software that reads a webpage out loud to them because reading may be difficult. The Library of Congress has been using the BrowseAloud program for a few years to help these patrons.[18]

Multiple Disabilities and Aging-Related Conditions

There are two other types of disabilities to consider. There are aging-related conditions that viewers may experience, which include issues with eyesight, hearing, mobility, or memory. Viewers may also have multiple disabilities, which can include any or all of the noted disability types. The assistive devices or technologies used by viewers with multiple disabilities or age-related conditions may be similar to those previously mentioned.

STRATEGIES

While it can seem like a daunting prospect, making archives' websites universally accessible is an achievable goal, even for a small organization. You just need time, some technical knowledge, and a lot of patience. To help make this process easier to implement, I have created a list of the most important changes you can make to your archives' website to help make it more universally accessible.

This list of changes is based on my experience working with accessibility and usability issues over the years, common accessibility and usability issues found in studies, audits of cultural and noncultural websites,[19] and major website accessibility guidelines, such as section 508 and the Web Content Access Guidelines (WCAG).[20] The WCAG are international, voluntary, technical guidelines created by the Web Accessibility Initiative (WAI) of the World Wide Web Consortium (W3C) in 1999 and updated in 2008. Most private entities and major governments around the world use these guidelines as the base for their website accessibility policies or legislation.

The following changes can apply to any archives or special collections website, whether it is made from the simplest HTML/CSS code or uses a content management system (CMS), such as Drupal or WordPress. These can also apply to the most basic website or one that has an online catalogue or search interface, digitized or born-digital materials, or information conveyed via text.

Improve Image Comprehension

Almost all webpages use images. They can be part of the webpage design or part of the content, including digital and digitized images of archival photographs, objects, or manuscripts. Some users will deliberately turn off the images in their Internet browsers because they have a slow or expensive Internet connection. Other users can't see images because they are blind or have very little functional sight. These viewers may use a screen-reader device or software on their computers to "read" the webpage for them. A great video demonstrating how a person uses a screen reader ("Screen Reader Demo 1") is available on YouTube.[21]

If someone can't see images, they need alternate descriptions of them in text format. Without alternate descriptions they can get confused or frustrated by not knowing what the image is representing or why it was put on the webpage so every image used on a webpage, no matter its function, needs a properly described "alt" or "alternate text" attribute in the image's HTML code. This "alt" is crucial because it provides viewers who can't see the image with text that explains its content and purpose.

How do you create an "alt" attribute with a proper description of the image? First, look at the importance of the image. What is its purpose? Is it just a decorative image? Is it crucial to the understanding of the website or the webpage? Does it provide context or content for the viewer?

If the image is just decorative or does not add any context or content, then the viewer who can't see it needs to know that he can skip it. To do this, use an empty "alt" attribute to tell the screen-reader software or device and viewers who can't see images to skip it. The following bolded code is what the empty "alt" looks like:

```
<ext>
<img src="not_important_image.jpg" alt="" width="1" height="1">.
</ext>
```

Many images are important for the content or context of a webpage or website, such as a logo; search button; or digital image of an archival photograph, object, or manuscript. For these, the viewer must be given a brief but accurate description in the alt attribute.

Here is an example of a recommended "alt" attribute description for the image of the Smithsonian Institution's logo: <img src="DG5467.jpg" alt="Smithsonian Institution logo" width="1" height="1">. This is brief and accurate, unlike this example, which is unnecessarily wordy: <img src="DG5467.jpg" alt="this is a yellow sun with alternating straight and curved rays within a blue circle and it is the logo from the Smithsonian Institution" width="1" height="1">.

If your image is a complex photograph or document, then your "alt" description becomes more complex. It may not be possible to sum up an archival item in a few words. Thus, I recommend that you provide a very brief description of the item in the "alt" and then provide a more detailed description of it in the text near that image, perhaps in a caption underneath it. Just do your best to describe complex images with "alts" and text, and know that this description will help all viewers, whether they can see them or not.

You should check all the images on your website to make sure that they have "alts" and they are properly described. Two of the best free online checkers are the Web Developer plug-in for the Firefox browser and the Lynx Viewer. [22]

Provide Clear Structure in Webpages

What if you picked up a book and it had no title or chapter headings? All you would see are paragraphs of text with no context or structure. This would be very confusing. This is what a person who is blind experiences with her screen reader when it "reads" webpages that don't include specified headings, which equate to the title and chapter headings of a book. These viewers require headings in the webpage code because they help provide the context and structure of that webpage.

In the HTML code of a webpage, the heading code is put around the titles, subtitles, or headings. The most important heading is denoted as <H1>, and this is usually the title of the webpage. The second-most important heading is denoted by <H2>, and then it goes down in importance from <H3> to <H6>. The key to headings is placing them in the proper hierarchical order, from top to bottom and from <H1> to <H6>.

For most sighted viewers, headings and their order don't matter. They can rely on seeing the entire page and the visual cues given by the structure, format, and context of the titles, subtitles, and headings on it. However, headings and their proper order are crucial to screen-reader users because many of them use a headings shortcut list as soon as they come to a webpage. This headings shortcut list shows all the headings on that page in the order they appear on the page from top to bottom. When reading that list, the screen-reader user knows that an <H1> is supposed to be used for the most important heading, <H2> the second-most important one, and so on. So if you use the headings out of order, such as <H6> for the title and <H1> for a subtitle, it confuses the user.

The headings shortcut list is a popular tool because it provides a very quick idea of the context and content of a webpage before reading or listening to the entire thing. This saves users a lot of time. Again, a useful video for seeing how a screen-reader user may interact with headings on a webpage ("Jaws Headings") is available on YouTube. [23]

You should check the headings in your website to make sure they are present and in a logical order. Again, there are two free and useful online checkers. The first is the Firefox plug-in called Fangs. [24] It emulates a screen reader and includes the headings shortcut list. The second is a very robust online checker that includes a headings check, and it is called the Functional Accessibility Evaluator (FAE). [25]

Provide Clear Structure for Word Documents

Some archives use Word documents on their websites for finding aids, transcripts of audio or video materials, or displaying born-digital or digitized images of archival materials.

When you create a Word document, it usually has a title, and often it has subtitles or headings. This structure is very similar to a webpage or a book that has a title, chapters, and content. Using headings in the proper order is just as important in Word documents as it was in web pages and is based on the same principle discussed in the previous section. To create headings in Word, you need to push a button in the "Styles" toolbar area to convert text into the appropriate heading level. There are many versions of Word, so consult the "Help" feature in your particular Word product for assistance on how to create headings.

One difference between headings on websites and in Word documents is that you can't see the heading codes (<H1>, <H2>, etc.) in the Word interface. There are two ways you can check the headings in your Word document. The first is to click every possible heading and watch whether it shows up as a heading in the "Style" toolbar area. The second, and easiest, method is to create a table of contents for the document, as it is formed by using the heading styles. By checking your headings, you can make sure they are present and in the proper order. Another benefit is that, if you create a PDF file from a Word document in which you have used proper headings, they should transfer to the PDF document.

Provide Clear Structure for PDF Documents

Many archives use PDF documents on their websites for finding aids, forms, instructions, audio or video transcripts, or born-digital or digitized materials. A PDF can be created from scratch, converted from a Word document, or created from other sources. No matter how a PDF is created, it can be made more accessible by adding tags for viewers with visual disabilities who use screen readers or screen-magnifying software programs.

Tags act like signposts that point to different parts of the structure of the PDF document, such as paragraphs, tables, images, links, and so on. A title tag would be used to indicate the title of the document, the paragraph tag indicates a paragraph, and so on. You can also have heading tags to indicate the kinds of headings discussed for Word documents and webpages.

For most sighted viewers, PDF tags are not necessary. However, these tags are crucial for people using screen readers and some people using screen magnifiers because they make the user aware of the document's context and structure. Without them, these viewers would likely experience a confusing jumble of content, again similar to reading a book without titles, chapters, or paragraphs.

How can you create tags? Fortunately, the popular PDF software, Adobe Acrobat Pro and Acrobat XI Pro, can tag an entire document in seconds by pressing one or two buttons. As noted, if you are converting a Word document into a PDF, you can create tags easily as the document is being converted. There are many versions of Adobe Acrobat Pro, so consult the "Help" feature in your particular product for assistance on how to add tags to your document and how to check them. You can also look at WebAIM's PDF-tagging page for directions.[26] WebAIM has been a trusted and respected source for accessibility resources since 1999.

Tagging may be easy to do, but it is not an exact science, especially on complex documents. In some cases, you may have to tag the document; complete an accessibility check; and then manually change, add, or delete certain tags. If you want to check your existing PDF documents to see if they are tagged, consult the "Help" feature in your specific Adobe Acrobat Pro product for instructions.

Improve Website Link Visibility

Almost all web pages use links, which are used to go to downloadable documents, images, other webpages on the same site, or a third-party website. These links have another use that few people know about: They also function as anchors or guides.

Some users with physical disabilities, visual disabilities, or cognitive disabilities find using a mouse either difficult or impossible. Instead, they use the keyboard and usually use the tab key to navigate the webpage. The tab key uses the links on the page as anchors or guides as it moves from the top to the bottom of the page. If the links on the page don't change in a visual way when the tab key hits them, users with sight disabilities can easily become disoriented. These users rely on these visual cues to show them where they are on the page.

Luckily, there is a very easy fix for this issue. You can add a snippet of code to your links called a focus state. This code gets added into the CSS file or code, which usually holds all the design information for your website, including the colors, sizes, underlines, and so on for all your links. The focus state code tells the Internet browser to highlight the link when the tab key clicks on it. The most common focus link highlight is a thin border or different background that comes up when the link is tabbed.

There are two easy ways to see if you have the focus state enabled on your website links. Go to one of your webpages, and instead of using your mouse, use the tab key and tab through to the bottom of the page. If the focus has been enabled, you will see the links change as you tab through them. You can also open the CSS file or code and search for the word *focus*. If there is no focus, then you can add it to the CSS code. For an example of how the focus code is used and what it looks like, look at the CSS code from my website.[27]

Make Links More Descriptive

Many websites use phrases like *click here* or *here* as the text that indicates links. These generic link descriptions are problematic for many reasons. I can't count how many times I have clicked on a link that wasn't well described, only to discover that it led to unwanted content, pop-up windows, or downloadable files. As well, these generic link descriptions can cause confusion for many viewers, including those with visual, physical, or cognitive/neurological disabilities. For example, people who use screen-magnifying software need descriptive link text. They may be reading your webpage at 200-percent magnification, so they can only see tiny bits of the page at one time. If the link is not descriptive, they then have to take time clicking it to see what the link does, and this takes a while at that magnification. The same kinds of issues apply to those using screen readers for whom it's not a trivial activity to open a different screen and then have the reader interpret it.

However, there is a very easy way to fix this issue. When creating a link, the text used for it should indicate what content the link will provide when the user clicks it. The best way to create good link text descriptions is to view the links out of context. Why do I suggest this? Many screen-reader users use shortcuts (as previously discussed with the use of proper headers) to quickly get an idea of page content before having to "read" the entire page from top to bottom. One of these shortcut lists shows all the links on that page, taking all the links out of context. Here is how some generic link text descriptions might be presented on a webpage:

- Society of American Archivists Accessibility Working Group website — Click here
- SAA Newsletter — Click here

Here is what the screen-reader user would see for them in their link list:

- Click here
- Click here

If we make the more descriptive text the actual link, the screen reader reads everything that is underlined:

- Society of American Archivists Accessibility Working Group website
- SAA Newsletter in PDF format

You can see how the last example gives viewers a much better idea of what will happen if they click the link.

You can view your links in a shortcut list if you use the Firefox plug-in Fangs, as it is a screen-reader emulator. If you don't use Fangs, then you must go through your links manually, taking note of what text is actually used for links and replacing it as needed.

Improve Layout and Readability of Textual Content

There are two major issues often associated with using text on your website. The first involves the layout of the textual content. Many websites have text that appears in long blocks with many paragraphs without breaks, long sentences, and very little surrounding white space. I have had difficulty with many websites because the text on the page was like this and I found it overwhelming and hard to read. Viewers with cognitive, intellectual, or neurological disabilities may also find these text-heavy pages hard to read and understand.

There are many ways to improve the layout of your textual content. You can break up paragraphs into smaller sections with bold section headings for easy readability. Paragraphs can be made shorter, with only three to five sentences in each one, so that the paragraph itself only takes up three to six lines on the page. More white space can be added around the text, which makes it easier to read and focus on. For example, this chapter has margins around it, which gives it white space, or what I call "breathing room."

If you want to check the layout of your textual content, ask different testers to check it for you. It is best if a range of people with different abilities are chosen to do this testing. As well, you can also use the Flesch Reading Ease Test in Word to get an idea of readability.[28] This test bases its rating on the average number of syllables per word and words per sentence and then rates text on a one hundred–point scale. The higher the score, the easier it is to understand the document. For most standard files, you want the score to be between sixty and seventy. Please consult the help manual in your Word product for more details.

The second issue involves the text itself and whether it is understandable. The language used in your website text can cause problems for many users, so try to make your content clear and understandable for your particular audience. It can be difficult to know who your audience is, however, so you should aim for as broad a range of audiences as possible. If you can, avoid the use of unusual or complex words. You may also want to avoid using terms with meanings not often understood by those not familiar with archival research, such as *fonds*, *record group*, *series*, or *provenance*. If you do use these words, then you may want to provide definitions for them.

You should also be aware of your use of acronyms and abbreviations. Make sure they are all fully described so everyone can understand them. Fully described acronyms and abbreviations and clear language are especially important for viewers with cognitive disabilities, such as dyslexia. It is also recommended that you try to keep the reading level of your content to the average, which is an eighth-grade level.[29] The Flesch-Kincaid Grade Level Test is included in Word products and can provide you with an assessment of the reading level of your text.

Improve Audio and Video Accessibility

Many archives use video or audio elements on their websites for such materials as oral histories, films, and audio recordings. These elements can be problematic for viewers who are deaf, deafened, or hard of hearing, as they may not be able to hear audio or video tracks. As well, viewers with visual disabilities may not be able to see your videos. In order to make video and audio files more universally accessible, try to use alternate methods of providing the same information that is in the video or audio.

It is highly recommended that you always provide a text transcript of your audio or video content. It is best if this can be presented right next to or under the audio or video file on the webpage. Some text transcripts can be very long, and even though this can make for a lot of text, it is still recommended. You may choose to have the text transcript on a different page from the audio/video content. If this is the case, it is crucial that the link to the text transcript be very clear and descriptive. All viewers can use this text transcript, even if they can see or hear the audio or video presentations. In fact, many may prefer the transcript, as it allows one to save time by not having to listen to an entire presentation in order to get one small piece of information from it.

If possible, it is recommended that you also caption your audio and video content. Captions allow viewers to read the content of the audio or video, right in the video or audio window. Captions may be used by many viewers, most especially those with auditory disabilities. If you use YouTube to present your audio or videos files, you can easily add closed captioning. Consult the YouTube "Help" section for further instructions. Keep in mind that this captioning can be flawed, so always test it. If you don't use YouTube and want to create captions yourself, please refer to the WebAIM website for expert recommendations on software and techniques.[30]

Finally, you can also create a sign language version of your audio and video materials. This is very useful for viewers who are deaf or deafened, as they may have learned sign language as their first language. The British Museum and Whitney Museum of American Art have successfully used sign language and captioned videos.[31]

There are no tools to test for audio and video accessibility, so you must check all materials manually and use testers if possible.

CONCLUSION

This chapter is only an introduction to the challenges involved with making archives websites universally accessible to all. The next step is to start talking with other archivists about universal accessibility, join or create accessibility groups in your archival associations, and start a conversation with local organizations that work with and support people with disabilities. Ask these local organizations questions and develop a relationship with them. As well, ask them if they can help you find people of all abilities who would be willing to test your website, for example as part of a focus group. If you are at a university or college, contact the department that supports members of the university community with disabilities. Listen to those who may experience challenges with your website, and ask lots of questions. This is how we make our websites universally accessible! As Tim Berners-Lee said, the power of the web is in its universality, and archivists must harness this power.

Lisa Snider *is the electronic records archivist at the Harry Ransom Center at the University of Texas at Austin.*

NOTES

1. "World Wide Web Consortium Launches International Program Office for Web Accessibility Initiative: Government, Industry, Research and Disability Organizations Join Forces to Promote Accessibility of the Web," *World Wide Web Consortium*, October 22, 1997, www.w3.org/Press/IPO-announce.

2. World Health Organization and the World Bank, "World Report on Disability," *World Health Organization*, 2011, www.who.int/disabilities/world_report/2011/report/en.

3. U.S. Census Bureau, *Americans with Disabilities: 2005*, December 2008, www.census.gov/prod/2008pubs/p70-117.pdf.

4. "SAA ARMT/RMRT Joint Working Group on Accessibility in Archives and Records Management," *Society of American Archivists*, accessed September 17, 2013, www2.archivists.org/groups/amrtrmrt-working-group-on-accessibility.

5. "Question—What is the difference between a person who is 'deaf,' 'Deaf,' or 'hard of hearing'?," *National Association of the Deaf*, accessed September 17, 2013, www.nad.org/issues/american-sign-language/community-and-culture-faq.

6. "SAA Core Values Statement and Code of Ethics," *Society of American Archivists*, accessed September 17, 2013, www2.archivists.org/statements/saa-core-values-statement-and-code-of-ethics. Principle 3 of the Association of Canadian Archivists' code of ethics states, "Archivists encourage and promote the greatest possible use of the records in their care." ("Code of Ethics," *Association of Canadian Archivists*, accessed October 20, 2013, http://archivists.ca/content/code-ethics).

7. Nicholas Taylor, "Designing Preservable Websites, Redux," *Library of Congress: The Signal: Digital Preservation*, February 6, 2012, http://blogs.loc.gov/digitalpreservation/2012/02/designing-preservable-websites-redux.

8. Ibid.

9. "National Federation of the Blind Files Complaint against Penn State," *National Federation of the Blind*, November 12, 2010, https://nfb.org/node/1026.

10. Max Freund, "UI Eyes More Accessible Website," *The Daily Iowan*, November 29, 2010, www.dailyiowan.com/2010/11/29/Metro/20210.html.

11. Keila Szpaller, "Disabled UM Students File Complaint over Inaccessible Online Courses," *Missoulian*, September 18, 2012, http://missoulian.com/news/local/disabled-um-students-file-complaint-over-inaccessible-online-courses/article_d02c27ac-0145-11e2-bc26-001a4bcf887a.html.

12. Elizabeth E. Clarke and Luke Ashworth, "Web-Based Accessibility under the ADA after Recent Netflix Decision," *Lexology*, August 6, 2012, www.lexology.com/library/detail.aspx?g=91db17f4-4a6a-4113-83b4-f375ef5ea8f9; Shannon K. Murphy, "Americans with Disabilities Act (ADA) and Accessible Online Video Requirements," *3PlayMedia*, June 13, 2013, www.3playmedia.com/2013/06/13/the-americans-disability-act-ada-accessible-online-video-requirements. The Department of Justice always felt websites were included as per "New Rules Will Require Websites to Be ADA Accessible," *Thompson Information Services*, April 28, 2010, www.thompson.com/public/newsbrief.jsp?cat=EMPLOYLAW&id=2809.

13. Brian Muse, "Does Your Business Have a Website? Get Ready for New ADA Regulations," *ADA Musings*, July 16, 2013, http://adamusings.com/2013/07/16/new-ada-web-regulations-coming.

14. Laurie Monsebraaten, "Blind Woman Says Federal Websites Discriminate against the Visually Impaired," *Thestar.com*, September 19, 2010, www.thestar.com/news/gta/2010/09/19/blind_woman_says_federal_websites_discriminate_against_the_visually_impaired.html; "Blind Woman Wins Case against Federal Government," *CBCNews*, November 29, 2010, www.cbc.ca/news/canada/blind-woman-wins-case-against-federal-government-1.956042; Gil Zvulony, "Web Accessibility Law in Canada," *Zvulony and Co.*, December 1, 2010, http://zvulony.ca/2010/articles/internet-law/web-accessibility.

15. Accessibility Advisory Council, "Accessibility Legislation Introduced in Manitoba," *Disabilities Issues Office*, April 24, 2013, www.gov.mb.ca/dio/aac/index.html.

16. "Standards sur l'accessibilité du Web," *Quebec Secrétariat du Conseil du trésor*, July 20, 2012, www.tresor.gouv.qc.ca/en/ressources-informationnelles/standards-sur-laccessibilite-du-web; "Status of Web Accessibility in Canada," *Soaring Eagle Communications*, 2005, www.webaccessibility.biz/canada.htm.

17. Access ON, "A Guide to the Integrated Accessibility Standards Regulation," *Ontario Ministry of Community and Social Services*, July 2012, www.mcss.gov.on.ca/documents/en/mcss/accessibility/iasr_guidelines/complete_guidelines.pdf.

18. "Web Site Access," *Library of Congress*, accessed September 18, 2013, www.loc.gov/access/web.html.

19. There are many studies, but the most well-known one is Helen Petrie, Neil King, and Fraser Hamilton, "Accessibility of Museum, Library and Archive Websites: The MLA Audit," *City University London*, 2005, www.jodiawards.org.uk/domains/jodiawards.org.uk/local/media/downloads/MLA_web_accessibility_audit.pdf. For a list of studies related to libraries until 2007, see Peter Brophy and Jenny Craven, "Web Accessibility," *Library Trends* 55, no. 4 (2007), 950–72.

20. Section 508 is currently being updated and will resemble WCAG 2.0, but for the latest version, see "Section 508 Standards Guide," *Section508.gov*, accessed September 18, 2013, www.section508.gov/section-508-standards-guide. See also "Web Content Accessibility Guidelines (WCAG) 2.0," *W3C*, December 11, 2008, www.w3.org/TR/WCAG20. Accessed January 28, 2014.

21. "Screen Reader Demo 1," YouTube video, 9:32, posted by uncweb, October 20, 2011, www.youtube.com/watch?v=92pM6hJG6Wo.

22. "Lynx Viewer Tool," *Yellowpipe*, accessed January 28, 2014, www.delorie.com/web/lynxview.html; Chrispederick, "Web Developer 1.2.5," *Add-ons*, accessed September 18, 2013, https://addons.mozilla.org/en-US/firefox/addon/web-developer.

23. "Jaws Headings," YouTube video, 1:46, posted by alfacord, June 23, 2009, www.youtube.com/watch?v=mqVMM5_GB6F.

24. Peter Krantz, "Fangs Screen Reader Emulator 1.0.8," *Add-Ons*, accessed September 18, 2013, https://addons.mozilla.org/en-us/firefox/addon/fangs-screen-reader-emulator.

25. Illinois Center for Information Technology and Web Accessibility, "Functional Accessibility Evaluator 1.1," *Functional Accessibility Evaluator 1.1: University of Illinois at Urbana – Champaign*, accessed September 18, 2013, http://fae.cita.uiuc.edu.

26. "PDF Accessibility," *WebAIM*, accessed September 17, 2013, http://webaim.org/techniques/acrobat/acrobat.

27. The CSS file with the focus code, is found at "style.css," *Lisa Snider*, accessed October 7, 2013, http://lisasnider.ca/sites/default/files/color/pixture_reloaded-437d07d9/style.css?z.

28. "Test Your Document's Readability," *Office*, accessed September 18, 2013, http://office.microsoft.com/en-us/word-help/test-your-document-s-readability-HP010148506.aspx.

29. In this article they recommend fourth- to fifth-grade level for people with cognitive disabilities. That can be hard to achieve in archival websites. See "Making Materials Useful for People with Cognitive Disabilities," *Southwest Educational Development Laboratory*, 2004, www.ncddr.org/products/researchexchange/v08n03/2_materials.html.

30. Ibid.

31. For examples of these videos, see "Channel: British Sign Language (BSL)—Room 4: Egyptian Sculpture," *The British Museum*, accessed September 18, 2013, www.britishmuseum.org/channel/object_stories/bsl/room_4_egyptian_sculpture/video_rosetta_stone.aspx; "Vlog: Paul Thek: Diver, A Retrospective," *Whitney Museum of American Art*, accessed September 18, 2013, http://whitney.org/WatchAndListen/Artists?play_id=367.

ELEVEN

No *Ship of Fools*

A Digital Humanities Collaboration to Enhance Access to Special Collections

Jennie Levine Knies, University of Maryland

The term *digital humanities* is now ubiquitous in academia and related fields; in 2011, *New York Times* blogger Stanley Fish noted that "upward of 40 sessions" at the 2012 meeting of the Modern Language Association meeting were devoted to "digital humanities."[1] Whether digital humanities is a lasting trend or a passing phenomenon, libraries as well as archives and special collections departments are exploring how to best accommodate and participate in these new initiatives. Over a two-month period in summer 2013, six prominent universities posted to the American Library Association JobLIST library jobs with *digital humanities* either in the title or prominent in the job description.[2]

Wikipedia provides the most basic definition of *digital humanities*: "an area of research, teaching, and creation concerned with the intersection of computing and the disciplines of the humanities."[3] This case study traces the long roots of the University of Maryland (UMD) Libraries' Katherine Anne Porter Correspondence and Digital Edition project, a digital humanities collaboration between librarians in special collections, scholars, technologists, and humanists from the Maryland Institute for Technology in the Humanities (MITH). Although the project is still ongoing, our experience shows how the use of technology by librarians and archivists to improve reference and access and to assist in teaching and instruction melds perfectly with a digital humanist's desire to use technology for analysis and demonstrates that libraries and archives can actively participate in and even "own" digital humanities projects.

Founded in 1999, the MITH is UMD's digital humanities center. Jointly supported by the UMD Libraries and the UMD College of Arts and Humanities, MITH "engages in collaborative, interdisciplinary work at the intersection of technology and humanistic inquiry" and specializes in "text and image analytics for cultural heritage collections, data curation, digital preservation, linked data applications, and data publishing."[4] Since its inception, MITH has provided UMD Libraries' staff with exposure to digital humanities work and actively encouraged UMD Libraries' staff to think beyond traditional curatorial activities with regards to archival and manuscript collections. It is this close relationship between the UMD Libraries and MITH over the past decade that laid the groundwork for the planning and implementation of the Katherine Anne Porter Correspondence and Digital Edition.

PLANNING

The first truly collaborative project between MITH and special collections at the UMD Libraries was the creation of ArchivesUM (http://digital.lib.umd.edu/archivesum). Starting in 2000 I began exploring methods to convert the UMD Libraries' archival finding aids into Encoded Archival Description (EAD). At the time tools such as the Archivists' Toolkit did not exist, and the libraries' archival staff was not interested in learning XML. The search for a form-based, user-friendly solution led to the creation of a Microsoft Access database into which archivists and student employees with no knowledge of EAD tags or structure could enter finding aid data.[5] We reached an impasse, however, and were unable to extract the data from Microsoft Access and convert it into an EAD-valid XML file. Dr. Susan Schreibman, then assistant director at MITH, volunteered project management and developer time to solve the extraction problem and also to develop an online interface and a tool for ingesting EAD XML into the system. The benefit for the UMD Libraries was the creation of a full-fledged archival management and delivery system, and the benefit for MITH was experience in applying techniques created to accommodate the Text Encoding Initiative (TEI) with a different type of XML.

The ArchivesUM collaboration opened a dialog between UMD librarians and Schreibman, and in 2004 Schreibman sought the assistance of myself (then curator of historical manuscripts) and Dr. Ruth M. (Beth) Alvarez (then curator of literary manuscripts) while planning a course for the UMD iSchool entitled "Creating Digital Repositories: Theory and Practice." We developed two projects based on different types of manuscript materials: correspondence and poetry. The students in the course formed two teams, each working on a distinct digital project from start to finish. The first project used the Sterling Family papers, a collection of sixty-two Civil War–era letters primarily written by Civil War Union officer's wife Tillie Farquhar Sterling. I identified the collection based on size and demand and spoke to the class about possible desirable outcomes. Researchers frequently requested copies of Civil War–era materials, and the 150th anniversary of the start of the Civil War was on the horizon. I wanted a model project to serve as a pilot for additional projects or to help in preparing a grant application. Students in the course transcribed the letters and then encoded them using TEI, working through issues surrounding metadata, controlled vocabularies, and display.[6] They also built an interface by which researchers could access the letters.

The second project, centered on the Elsa von Freytag-Loringhoven papers, a literary manuscript collection, was a more obvious precursor to the Katherine Anne Porter Correspondence and Digital Edition. The Baroness Elsa von Freytag-Loringhoven Digital Library featured seven poems by Freytag-Loringhoven, the German-born but American-based poet and visual and performance artist best known as a pivotal figure of the New York Dada movement.[7] The UMD Libraries acquired the collection with the papers of another twentieth-century writer and artist, Djuna Barnes, in 1973. Working closely with Alvarez and making use of previous work of graduate students in the English department, the iSchool students not only transcribed and made available the poems but also made use of an analysis tool called the Versioning Machine, enabling comparison of versions of texts created by Freytag-Loringhoven. The Versioning Machine relies on TEI markup. Its framework combines the two major editorial models, facsimile and critical, giving readers opportunities to engage with different states of the text. It allows readers to view a TEI-encoded critical edition (a "diplomatic witness") alongside a scanned image of the original page; view two, three, or all diplomatic witnesses side by side; or compare the facsimile images to each other without reference to the diplomatic version(s).[8] The iSchool students used the transcriptions created by the English graduate students as the basis for their own encoding of the poems and incorporated the relevant English graduate student reflective essays into their projects. Both course projects were successful and are still maintained by the UMD Libraries. We learned many lessons through working with these classes, including how to think beyond basic access to digitized archival material and the benefits of collaborating with scholars in order to determine the most effective use scenario for collections.

In 2005 Schreibman became assistant dean and head of digital collections and research at the UMD Libraries. Alvarez and Schreibman sought to continue their collaboration by submitting a grant proposal to the National Endowment for the Humanities (NEH) to create a more complete

Elsa von Freytag-Loringhoven "Digital Archive." The proposal sought to digitize Freytag-Loringhoven's personal papers, including the poetry, her correspondence, and an autobiography, to make use of the Versioning Machine to allow for visual comparison of the different drafts of the poetry, to establish an online journal to support study of the work of Freytag-Loringhoven and her circle, and to create a blog to provide a space for less-mediated community involvement. Alvarez and Schreibman outlined two primary goals for the project, both of which addressed the needs of archivist and scholar. The first goal was to make the Freytag-Loringhoven papers more easily and usefully accessible. The NEH had previously funded the microfilming of the Barnes and Freytag-Loringhoven papers between 2002 and 2004, and the UMD Libraries established policies for sharing the microfilm with scholars around the world. Alvarez, however, recognized that the microfilm did not always provide all of the information necessary for scholarship. Freytag-Loringhoven created her work on paper of various sizes, quality, and color, making use of black as well as colored pencil and ink, none of which was accurately captured on black-and-white microfilm. In addition, Alvarez was aware that scholars researching and publishing about Freytag-Loringhoven originated in a number of different disciplines, not only literature and history but also art history, women's studies, and theater and performance studies. Therefore, the second project goal was to "provide opportunities for contemporary interdisciplinary scholarship and creativity that will draw on, interrogate, and augment the core corpus."[9] The Internet provided the perfect framework for this type of new, digital scholarship.

The NEH did not fund the 2005 grant; the major critique involved Freytag-Loringhoven's relative obscurity as a subject, and Alvarez and Schreibman resubmitted in 2006, retitling the application "Elsa von Freytag-Loringhoven Digital Archive and Collaboratory." They had used the term *collaboratory* in the narrative of the earlier grant and chose to emphasize it a second time In the year between the grant applications, *Web 2.0* had become a common term, and new tools and websites, such as Flickr and Del.icio.us, that allowed not only for the sharing of digital assets but also for collaboration and interaction were gaining in popularity. Alvarez and Schreibman also refined the original goals of the grant, indicating that a central goal was "to serve as a model for a new generation of digital archives."[10] Without using a term like *social tagging*, they envisioned a "virtual research space" where members of the academic, library, and museum communities could "leverage the combined knowledge of their constituencies to reduce the cost of this aspect [creating metainformation] of content creation, [so that] far more content will have the potential to be available in digital form."[11]

When the NEH once again did not grant funding, Alvarez and Schreibman turned their attention elsewhere, although Alvarez continued to encourage scholars to make use of the Freytag-Loringhoven papers for projects. In 2008 UMD dissertation candidate Tanya Clement created "In Transition: Selected Poems by the Baroness Elsa von Freytag-Loringhoven," as part of her dissertation, *The Makings of Digital Modernism*.[12] "In Transition" sought to explore Clement's theory of textual performance, in which a text in performance can comprise multiple versions in manuscript and print, various notes and letters, and comments of contemporaries or current readers, plus the element of performance. When a text is "in performance," it is within a constant circulation of networked relationships, and the making of meaning is in a constant state of transition. It is always a live performance. The Versioning Machine was a perfect tool to illustrate this theory.

Clement had worked as a project manager and graduate assistant for MITH and as a graduate assistant for Schreibman in the UMD Libraries. Because Clement was using content owned by the UMD Libraries in her project, we worked together to identify methods of collaboration so that Clement's project could become a part of the UMD Libraries' digital collections. The project exposed many of the limitations of a standard digital repository when working with a digital humanist. The UMD Libraries' online digital collections (http://digital.lib.umd.edu), launched in 2005 and built using the Fedora architecture, aimed from the beginning to do more than simply provide access to digitized objects. Schreibman and her staff designed the repository both to accommodate thematic collection interfaces and to allow for serendipitous discovery across thematic collections. A crosswalk and application was installed to allow for harvesting of the metadata from the collections into other databases, such as OCLC WorldCat. However, the ability to use and manipulate the actual digital content was very restricted, primarily due to archivists' concerns over control of materials. Downloading large amounts of content or even providing a structure that would allow those outside of the UMD Libraries to easily manipulate content were not possible. This required extensive work by Clement to understand the repository architecture and close collaboration with UMD Libraries' staff to ensure that her interface designs would work within the confines of our system. It was clear that this was not the most efficient way to provide material to a digital humanities scholar.

After receiving her doctorate, Clement became the associate director of the Digital Cultures and Creativity Program at UMD, a curriculum aimed at engaging undergraduates in emerging technologies.[13] She continued to collaborate with the UMD Libraries, approaching us for collections to incorporate into her course projects. Clement and her students expanded Clement's dissertation work by exploring how one might conceive of an "edition" in a digital environment. Using the open-source tool Omeka as a development platform, Clement's students transcribed, encoded, and "exhibited" special collections content. Clement continued this exploration when she left UMD in 2011 to join the University of Texas's School of Information, working remotely with us to develop these course projects, primarily using 768 letters between Katherine Anne Porter and her sister, Gay Porter Holloway, as the test bed for her class "Special Topics in Information Science: Introduction to Digital Humanities." The goal of the project was to determine the most innovative interfaces and systems and the best standards for accessing and sustaining the collection has a whole. Course activities included transcribing letters, encoding in TEI, creating metadata for searching, retrieval, and indexing and designing a presentation interface.

IMPLEMENTATION

The UMD Libraries is home to the primary archive for author Katherine Anne Porter (1890–1980). [14] Porter is known primarily for her short stories and novel, *Ship of Fools*. She was awarded a Pulitzer Prize and the National Book Award in 1966 for *The Collected Stories of Katherine Anne Porter* (see figure 11.1). Her personal papers reflect her interests in writing, travel, politics, and current events and also document her private life. The collection includes correspondence, notes and drafts for her works, publications, legal documents, and financial records. It also includes more than 1,500 photographs from her personal collection, dating from the 1890s to 1979.

Scholars from around the world visit the UMD Libraries to use the Porter papers for research. Alvarez is herself a Porter scholar. She became an expert with the papers while working on her 1990 doctoral dissertation *Katherine Anne Porter and Mexican Art*. Three years after completing her dissertation, Alvarez, who also holds a master of library science degree, joined the UMD Libraries faculty. As both scholar and curator, she has always been a strong supporter and instigator of new and interesting uses of Porter's rich legacy. In the predigital world, these included the publication of critical essays, the creation and mounting of exhibits, the organization of public events and conferences, and the acquisitions of additional Porter materials and complementary manuscript collections. One of Alvarez's first activities as curator was to embark upon an NEH-funded microfilming project of the collection, which was completed between 1994 and 1997.

In 2012, Clement, Alvarez, Trevor Muñoz (assistant dean for digital humanities research at the UMD Libraries and associate director of MITH), and I cosupervised a capstone project for University of Texas graduate student Wendy Hagenmaier. Hagenmaier had participated in Clement's 2011 course and was interested in further pursuing the question of what constituted a "digital scholarly edition." Her final report, "Exploring the Future of Digital Scholarly Editions: A Case Study of the

Figure 11.1.   Katherine Anne Porter in hat with magnolia corsage, May 15, 1960, Hay Meadows, Rosemont, New Jersey. Back inscription, no. 1: "Taken by Paul in Barbara Wescott's garden on my 70th birthday." no. 2: "70th birthday/ 6/18/77/ R Beach." *Photo by Paul Porter. Special Collections, University of Maryland Libraries*

Letters of Katherine Anne Porter," which included interviews with librarians, archivists, and scholars, outlined many of the issues involved in creating a digital scholarly edition and provided insight into how these different professionals defined their roles in the world of digital archives. She identified three key areas where these professionals could combine efforts: the demand for the resources to build central digital repositories that are open, interdisciplinary, multimedia, and built to support cross-institutional projects; the continued need for resources at archives and libraries to produce and publish small and large curated data sets or scholarly editions and projects; and a sense that these products must circulate for peer review and remixing within a wider community that is

educated in the scholarly work these kinds of projects entail.[15] Using
Hagenmaier's report and its recommendations as a roadmap, we formed
a project team in fall 2012 to put together a formal project proposal for a
Katherine Anne Porter Correspondence and Digital Edition pilot.

Several organizational changes between 2011 and 2012 helped to
move this project forward. Alvarez retired in 2011 and, as a librarian
emerita, is able to devote time to this project. After Schreibman's departure in 2008, the UMD Libraries had moved the office of digital collections into special collections, appointing me as an interim manager. In
2009, the UMD Libraries appointed a new dean, who in turn hired an
associate dean for information technology (later "digital systems and stewardship"). Digital collections moved into the newly named digital systems and stewardship division and became two departments: digital programs and initiatives, a centralized unit headed by me and focused on
technology transfer, digital curation and preservation, and digital project
management, and a separate digital conversion and media reformatting
unit focused solely on digitization of images, text, audio, and video and
managed by Robin Pike. Special collections also reorganized, allowing
special collections librarian Joanne Archer to shift her focus entirely toward managing digital projects. In 2011, the UMD Libraries and MITH
hired Trevor Muñoz in a joint position between the libraries and MITH,
further solidifying the understanding of the UMD Libraries to the value
of the digital humanities on library work. A memorandum of understanding, revised and updated annually, outlines the details of the mutually beneficial relationship and includes a program by MITH to "provide
[digital humanities]–related training . . . to library staff" and stipulates
that the UMD Libraries will provide appropriate release time to allow
UMD Libraries staff to participate in digital humanities–related projects
with MITH.[16] These changes all converged to allow for the confidence
that embarking on such a project could be successful.

Intellectual property and funding also played crucial roles in starting
this project. In January 2011, the dean of the UMD Libraries officially
became one of the literary trustees of the estate of Katherine Anne Porter.
The literary trustees control the intellectual property residing in Porter's
published and unpublished work and have the authority to grant permission to make Porter's work available online. They also control the financial assets of the estate and can authorize use of funds for "charitable,
educational, literary and scientific purposes."[17] The project team approached the literary trustees with a proposal seeking start-up funding.
The proposal outlined a pilot project with the following elements and
goals:

- Formation of an advisory board including literary scholars and
  archivists as well as experts in digital humanities to assist the project team

- Selection of materials from Porter's correspondence whose copyright is controlled by the trustees of the literary estate, that are in stable condition, that are representative of the materials found in all of the libraries' Porter holdings, and that have significant scholarly content
- Digitization of the correspondence at a competitive cost, adhering to high technical standards while ensuring the safety of the valuable originals
- Development of an online interface to the collection informed by current research on best practices for the publication of digital editions
- Development of appropriate indexes, retrieval mechanisms, and other analytical tools attached to the online collection to support its ongoing curation

The pilot project proposed focusing on Porter's correspondence to her family, comprising almost 5,000 pages of material: 793 pages of letters from Porter to her older sister (representing 359 letters) and an additional 4,133 pages to various other members of her family. These selections represented a well-scoped pilot project to apply to an additional 30,000 pages of letters from Porter to other correspondents that might be digitized in the future.

The project team requested $13,672 for one year to support the initial phase of work. The UMD Libraries proposed to contribute $10,677 of staff time as a cost-share. The funding requested covered the cost of digitization, a research assistant, and several students, including one to focus on interface design. The literary trustees approved the funding, and in October 2012 the project began work in earnest. In the preceding months, we had been implementing several project management strategies and applied them to this project. The first task was for the project team to draft and approve a project charter, which outlined the specific objectives, scope, and stakeholders in the project, in more detail than the original proposal. The stated objectives for the project included creation of a scholarly digital edition, providing access and long-term preservation of the scholarly digital edition, and to be a model for other large-scale, comprehensive, digital preservation and access projects. The project charter also reiterated the justification for the project, detailed the resources needed, and clearly specified the components. For this project, the primary components include material selection, copyright and licensing, bibliographic data, file management, import into digital repository, quality control, digital preservation, website development, and access.

Perhaps the most useful aspect of the project charter is the section that clearly defines roles and responsibilities for each stakeholder. Earlier projects had failed to progress due to bottlenecks created from project members not clearly understanding their tasks. We are currently experimenting with the concept of assigning a project manager and a principal investigator for each project. These two roles fill crucial but very different leadership for the project. As project manager, Archer's role is concerned with the "how" and "when" questions relating to the project and consists of attending to practical matters, such as creating shared workspaces, creating to-do lists, coordinating meetings, writing the project plan, and tracking resources. As principal investigator, Muñoz focuses on the "what" and "why" questions relating to the project and remains focused on the big picture, articulating the benefits and requirements to those responsible for its implementation. As such, he is responsible for coordinating with all the internal and external stakeholders in defining the conditions for "success" — that is, by what specific criteria will the project be judged to have fulfilled the business goals for which it was created. The theory is that these two positions will serve as a check-and-balance system, allowing the project to remain true to its vision even if and when compromise becomes necessary. Although not formally listed as the principal investigator, Alvarez's role in visioning the project is very strong. Her task was to write the key text for the digital edition and lead the advisory board, whose primary role was to provide input on design and scholarly value of the digital edition.

Other stakeholders were assigned very specific tasks. Pike and her staff would coordinate all of the digitization and creation of optical character recognition (OCR), including communication with the vendor and quality-assurance-checking on materials returned. I would identify and retrieve all of the correspondence previously digitized as part of the earlier course projects, facilitate loading the new digital assets into the repository, advise on descriptive metadata, and ensure the long-term preservation of the digital content. For the most part, this type of work is part of our routine job descriptions.

A newly hired research assistant would coordinate the daily and descriptive tasks relating to the project, including identifying and preparing materials for digitization, assisting with the quality review upon return from the vendor, revising finding aids, and writing the occasional blog post or other public relations item for the project. Muñoz began experimentation with topic modeling and metadata exploration using a combination of Solr, Blacklight and some topic modeling utilities created by MITH in 2012. The graduate assistant to assist with the user interface design work will be hired in January 2014.

The project team communicates through Basecamp, project management software that provides the ability to preserve discussions, create to-do lists, assign tasks, take notes, and store files.[18] The project plan details the timeline for the project. At the time of writing, the fifth shipment of correspondence has been returned from the vendor. A total of eight shipments of correspondence has been digitized by and returned from the vendor. The digital assets will then be ingested into the UMD Libraries' digital collections, and Muñoz and the user interface student will spend the fall working on the design and presentation. The project team created a brief website (http://digital.lib.umd.edu/kap) to announce the work, and this site also serves as a placeholder for the final product when the project is complete.

RESULTS

I have described this project without perhaps elaborating on what constitutes a digital edition and what separates this from a cut-and-dry digitization project. So far, the description, with the digitization and ingestion into the UMD Libraries' digital repository, sounds straightforward and familiar to archival readers. By linking the digitized content to the archival finding aid, the project will provide researchers who desire the traditional archival practice of browsing through a collection at the folder and item level to recreate that practice in an online environment. In 2009 we took this exact approach when we digitized the five reels of preservation microfilm of Freytag-Loringhoven's papers. Researchers can access the Freytag-Loringhoven papers through links in the archival finding aid or by searching UMD's digital collections.[19] While researchers have complimented us on the increased availability of this collection, there are also limitations to this representation, including lack of full-text search, inability to download files (due to technical limitations imposed by the existing website interface), and—because of this—difficulty in pulling together content from different parts of the collection.

In contrast, a digital edition contains elements of interpretation and analysis that go beyond a traditional archival digitization project. To determine how to support these requirements, the project team identified some research questions to drive the work of the interface design, how the project would manifest to the public, and how we might measure its success. We are seeking answers to such basic questions as "Who are the users for these materials?" "What are their information needs?" and "How might a digital edition of these letters embedded in a larger library collection help them to complete their research?" What questions about Katherine Anne Porter's life might these letters illuminate, or more broadly, why read another person's letters at all? What questions about Porter's composition and literary work could we imagine pursuing? How will scholars read this correspondence—in pursuit of detailed facts or for deeply following a narrative—and how separable are these two potential uses? What questions do we have about the methods for representing materials like these in digital form, and how would the uses identified affect the interfaces? The answers to these questions remain to be seen. The advisory board has already speculated that the intrinsic ability of digital to allow for volume is an advantage—the two previously published volumes of edited letters comprise just under 400 letters combined (UMD holds approximately 30,000 pages of Porter's correspondence altogether). They posit that this project will allow researchers to develop their own narrative in a way that is not possible with the previously published edited volumes.

On a more practical level, this project allowed the UMD Libraries to take advantage of significant organizational change and develop new policies and procedures for project management and how special collections, digital systems and stewardship, and MITH might collaborate. It was during the course of this project that the idea of appointing a principal investigator and a project manager as two separate entities really developed. The identification and definition of these two roles is being used in all subsequent digital projects throughout the UMD Libraries. Establishing digitization workflows for large-scale manuscript digitization projects was another unexplored area for the UMD Libraries. As with microfilming projects, digitization projects require attention to detail and extensive prework and planning. It required collaboration to select a vendor, make metadata decisions, finalize file-name structures, solidify imaging requirements, and create a quality review process. The products of this project will serve as templates for others moving forward. Once again, defining roles and responsibilities was key to the success of this part of the project.

LESSONS LEARNED

Several challenges have already presented themselves with this project, and more promise to move to the forefront once work on the interface commences. For example, the project charter states that each letter will have its own unique uniform resource identifier (URI) to mark its home on the web. The UMD Libraries use the Handle System to assign unique, persistent identifiers to its digital objects.[20] A handle, while unique, consists of a relatively vague structure. Muñoz has requested that we investigate using "cool URIs" in order to facilitate linked data. *Linked data* refers to a set of best practices for publishing and connecting structured data on the web, and in this context Muñoz is envisioning that, in order to make this project useful to the largest number of people, it is necessary to provide the data about the letters, the people involved, the subjects, in such a way that it can be shared, referred to, and reused. For example, the handle for the illustration "Wheels are growing in rosebushes" by Freytag-Loringhoven is http://hdl.handle.net/1903.1/9095, which is hardly descriptive and does not conform to some of the recommendations about URI construction.[21] The URL http://digital.lib.umd.edu/image?pid=umd:69250 also points to the illustration. This is slightly more descriptive, as it indicates that the image is located at the digital.lib.umd.edu domain. It also references the UMD Libraries' repository's internal identification system by using the persistent identifier *umd:69250*. But the *image?pid=* portion of that string could change if the UMD Libraries modify how images or illustrations are disseminated on their website (in fact, the URL used to be http://www.lib.umd.edu/digital/image.php?pid=umd:69250). An example of a cool URI might be something like http://id.lib.umd.edu/freytag-loringhoven/69250.[22] The handles and a cool URI may not be mutually exclusive, but this question is one that the UMD Libraries had not considered prior to this project, and it may not be possible to implement this before the first iteration of the Katherine Anne Porter Correspondence and Digital Edition goes online.

A second and potentially controversial challenge on the horizon involves the level of accessibility of the digitized content, the design of the edition's interface, and whether there *will* be a locally designed digital edition interface. The digitized letters and their derivatives will live within the UMD Libraries' digital repository and be accessible at the very basic level via hyperlinks from the archival finding aids and through basic searches in digital collections. However, the UMD Libraries' digital collections' default interface does not currently provide a mechanism for viewing transcriptions and digital images side by side, easily downloading data, or doing full-text searches. In a July 2013 meeting, the advisory board indicated that these are three characteristics that they felt would add value to the content and make this digital edition truly special. They also suggested that the contents of the site be accessible via a timeline or chronology of Porter's life.[23] Prior to the advisory board meeting, Muñoz had already been concerned with different interface concepts and approaches, based partially on Hagenmeier's recommendations about sharing of data. In a December 2012 presentation to a UMD iSchool course, Muñoz had argued for building the project "website" through Wikipedia.[24] The argument for such an approach centers on the realities of what we know about how users access information (rarely directly through a library website) and the various sister tools that have been developed to interact with Wikipedia, such as Wikisource and Wikimedia Commons.[25] In a 2009 article in *The American Archivist,* Jenn Riley and Kelcy Shepherd wrote about shareable metadata, "This model of wide and unrestricted sharing is relatively new for archivists, who are accustomed to mediating access to archival collections."[26] While comfortable with the idea of enhancing Wikipedia articles, more elaborate and widespread sharing of the content itself is a concept that is still under discussion, although it seems as though it would be one experimental way for the UMD Libraries to further collaborate with and interact with scholars.

One area that was relatively new territory with the UMD Libraries was OCR. Most but not all of Porter's correspondence is typed, and we wanted to receive OCR files from the digitization vendor for these materials in order to enhance searchability. We asked for files in hOCR format because these additional outputs from the OCR engine contain valuable information about the location of regions of text on the page. Especially for typefaces where OCR performance is likely to be poor, having this topological information about the page can help us to target our transcription and correction efforts more effectively.[27] This information is valuable for supporting user interface behaviors and computational processing over and above the actual machine-readable text output of the OCR process alone. The initial pilot project only required OCR files and does not specify whether TEI or another encoding system might be used to enhance the content, so decisions about OCR had to be flexible. The OCR on the Porter correspondence to this point has been clear on typewritten letters with dark ink and much less precise on letters typed on onion-skin paper, which is very transparent. At the end of the project, we will evaluate the usefulness of the OCR and of the hOCR over a straight OCR text file. Our expectation is that some form of crowdsourcing might be employed to correct and update the errors in the OCR as well as to transcribe handwritten materials.

CONCLUSION

The Katherine Anne Porter Correspondence and Digital Edition project, although not complete at time of writing, has been a successful collaboration between librarians and digital humanists and demonstrates how libraries and archives can take a leading role in creating robust digital collections that serve the research needs of digital humanities scholars, while at the same time enhance discovery and access to all types of users. The project evolved from a series of successful outreach and instruction experiences with students and faculty at the University of Maryland to a well-developed scholarly project, aimed at both the student community and scholars worldwide.

Once the pilot is complete, we will have a model that can be applied as a template to future projects, either by building the Porter project or by testing our techniques and processes on other collections. By making this content widely available in a number of different venues and applications, we hope that the scholars will explore new ways to use the collections to answer their research questions and that they will continue to communicate with us and share their tools and techniques so that we can adapt our processes as necessary.

Jennie Levine Knies is manager, digital programs and initiatives, Digital Systems and Stewardship Division, University of Maryland Libraries.

NOTES

1. Stanley Fish, "The Old Order Changeth," *New York Times*, December 26, 2011, http://opinionator.blogs.nytimes.com/2011/12/26/the-old-order-changeth.

2. "ALA JobLIST," *American Library Association*, http://joblist.ala.org. Search performed on August 10, 2013, for keyword *digital humanities*.

3. "Digital Humanities," *Wikipedia*, accessed August 2, 2013, http://en.wikipedia.org/wiki/Digital_humanities. For a very thorough discussion of digital humanities, see Susan Schreibman, Ray Siemens, John Unsworth, eds., *Companion to Digital Humanities*, Blackwell Companions to Literature and Culture (Oxford: Blackwell, 2004), www.digitalhumanities.org/companion.

4. Maryland Institute for Technology in the Humanities, "About," *University of Maryland*, accessed August 2, 2013, http://mith.umd.edu/about.

5. For a complete history of ArchivesUM, see Jennie A. Levine, Jennifer Evans, and Amit Kumar, "Taming the 'Beast': An Archival Management System Based on EAD," *Journal of Archival Organization* 4, no. 3–4 (2007), 63–98, dx.doi.org/10.1300/J201v04n03_05.

6. *The Sterling Family Papers*, http://hdl.handle.net/1903.1/1204. 2004. Accessed August 1, 2013.

7. *Baroness Elsa von Freytag-Loringhoven Digital Library*, 2005, http://hdl.handle.net/1903.1/1205. Accessed August 31, 2013.

8. *Versioning Machine 4.0*, accessed August 2, 2013, http://v-machine.org.

9. Susan Schreibman and Ruth M. Alvarez, "Elsa von Freytag-Loringhoven Digital Archive," proposal to the National Endowment for the Humanities, Grants to Preserve and Create Access to Humanities Collections, July 15, 2005, University of Maryland Libraries.

10. Susan Schreibman and Ruth M. Alvarez, "Elsa von Freytag-Loringhoven Digital Archive and Collaboratory," proposal to the National Endowment for the Humanities, Grants to Preserve and Create Access to Humanities Collections, July 25, 2006, University of Maryland Libraries.

11. Ibid.

12. Tanya Clement, ed., *In-Transition: Selected Poem by the Baroness Elsa von Freytag-Loringhoven*, http://hdl.handle.net/1903.1/4945; and Tanya E. Clement, *The Makings of Digital Modernism: Rereading Gertrude Stein's* The Making of Americans *and Poetry by Elsa von Freytag-Loringhoven*, Ph.D. diss., University of Maryland, 2009, http://hdl.handle.net/1903/9160.

13. "Digital Culture and Creativity," *University of Maryland*, http://dcc.umd.edu. Accessed August 1, 2013.

14. "Katherine Anne Porter Papers," *ArchivesUM*, http://hdl.handle.net/1903.1/1532. Accessed August 1, 2013.

15. Tanya Clement, Wendy Hagenmaier, and Jennie Levine Knies, "Toward a Notion of the Archive of the Future: Impressions of Practice by Librarians, Archivists, and Digital Humanities Scholars," *Library Quarterly: Information, Community, Policy* 83, no. 2 (2012), 112–30.

16. Trevor Muñoz, *UMD Libraries and Maryland Institute for Technology in the Humanities (MITH), 2012 Agenda*, Memorandum of Understanding, University of Maryland, April 12, 2012.

17. Last will and testament, July 12, 1972 (filed October 2, 1980), Prince George's County, Maryland. Copy in possession of the University of Maryland Libraries.

18. Basecamp (http://basecamp.com) is a commercial software package. The lowest plan allows for ten projects at a cost of twenty dollars per month. It is an excellent tool for collaborating with different groups of people, especially across departments or organizations. Its weakness is document collaboration. For that purpose, the project team uses Google Drive or shares files on the UMD Libraries' local area network.

19. "Elsa von Freytag-Loringhoven Papers," *ArchivesUM*, http://hdl.handle.net/1903.1/1501. Accessed August 1, 2013.

20. *Handle System*, www.handle.net. Accessed August 1, 2013.

21. An excellent analysis of persistent URIs may be found in Interoperability Solutions for European Public Administrations, *D7.1.3—Study on Persistent URIs, with Identification of Best Practices and Recommendations on the Topic for the MSs and EC*, December 17, 2012, https://joinup.ec.europa.eu/sites/default/files/D7.1.3 - Study on persistent URIs_4.pdf.

22. Juha Hakala, "Persistent Identifiers—An Overview," *Standards in Metadata and Interoperability*, http://metadaten-twr.org/2010/10/13/persistent-identifiers-an-overview. October 13, 2010.

23. Katherine Anne Porter Correspondence and Digital Edition Advisory Board meeting, University of Maryland Libraries, College Park, Maryland, unpublished minutes, July 2, 2013.

24. Trevor Muñoz, *Katherine Anne Porter Correspondence Project: Design Concept*, unpublished presentation, December 2012.

25. "Wikipedia: Wikimedia Sister Projects," *Wikipedia*, https://en.wikipedia.org/wiki/Wikipedia:Wikimedia_sister_projects. Accessed August 1, 2013.

26. Jenn Riley and Kelcy Shepherd, "A Brave New World: Archivists and Shareable Descriptive Metadata," *The American Archivist* 72, no. 1 (Spring–Summer 2009), 91–112.

27. For an example of how other digital humanities projects use this information, note the highlighting behavior in New York Public Library's new Ensemble crowdsourcing application at http://ensemble.nypl.org/transcriptions/start.

TWELVE

Websites as a Digital Extension of Reference

*Creating a Reference and IT Partnership for Web
Usability Studies*

Sara Snyder and Elizabeth Botten, Archives of
American Art

When the Archives of American Art launched a robust new website in
2005—which was dynamically driven by our collections database and
consisted of tens of thousands of pages—it featured some level of description for all of our collections as well as thousands of digital surrogates. Since then, the website (aaa.si.edu) has continued to grow in scale
and complexity. The huge growth in our digital collections has led to a
similar expansion among the number and variety of our online visitors.
Though we had always considered ourselves a specialized repository
with a core audience of experienced academic researchers, our online
collections attracted a greater number of undergraduate students, casual
researchers, art enthusiasts, and genealogists, many of whom submit reference questions through our online form.

A successful website is a great help to reference staff; conversely, a
poorly organized or inaccurate one will result in repeat questions. The
ideal archives website should empower researchers to answer many of
the basic questions on their own so that reference staff can spend their
time working on the more complex or unique inquiries. From posting the
reading room hours to the findability of finding aids, making information

easy and obvious to access online spares reference staff from addressing questions that should be self-serve.

But how do we know if researchers are finding the information they need on our websites? How can we tell if they struggling to find what they need? User-centered design methods like usability testing complement the data we collect via surveys and web analytics. These techniques help us gauge success and stay focused on prioritizing those digital projects that give the greatest benefit to our audiences. Just as reference staff strive in our face-to-face interactions with patrons to be professional and empathetic, we want the same standards of service from our digital platforms.

Since 2007, the reference and web/IT departments at the Archives of American Art have been partnering to run an ongoing series of website usability studies on the Archives of American Art's website. The studies are focused on gathering pragmatic, actionable feedback that we can use to make the website more useful for our key audiences. We begin each round of testing by reviewing and drawing inspiration from real-life reference questions and comments submitted via the reference department's webform, then reformulating those inquiries as tasks for use during web usability tests. We conduct the tests on volunteer participants, while using software to record their participation for later analysis. Rather than detailing the specific findings of each study, this case study introduces our methodology, tells the story of how we got our program off the ground, and recounts some lessons learned from six years of user testing at a single repository. Instead of laying down a series of assertions about what "users" universally want, we feel strongly that each unique web interface merits its own set of usability tests in order to best inform the designers of that specific system. A result that pertained Archives of American Art's interface might not apply at a different repository with different audiences.

PLANNING

Traditionally, IT staff and reference staff have represented disparate ends of archival workflow—the backend and the frontline—with little cause for intense collaboration. To the public who use an archives' website, however, there is little distinction between one department and another; they simply want to find the answers they need quickly and easily. Responsibility for the design and maintenance of web-user interfaces typically falls to IT staff, but reference specialists are the ones who often possess the most profound understanding of the archives' audiences. How could the Archives of American Art create a sensible method of incorporating the expertise and perspective of the reference archivists deep into our web development process? It required a shift in thinking about what reference does and how their work comprises a fundamental part of the web-user experience.

The sum of a users' perceptions, emotions, and responses as they interact with your organization online comprise their user experience (or UX, in web parlance). This begins the moment your website comes up in their search results and they make the choice to click through to your site. User experience includes how people feel about the way that your site renders in the browser, its aesthetic, its speed and responsiveness, search results, ease of navigation, and accessibility of finding aids and digital collections, all the way to how easy or difficult it is to contact your staff (if needed). The experience is shaped by the choices people make in creating the site, from the indexable keywords archivists put into their folder titles to the technology the IT team selects to power the main website search box.

In order to improve the online user experience, every department and staff member must have an awareness of how his or her work connects them to the end user. One of usability testing's great strengths as a research methodology is not only how efficiently it helps you prioritize future design improvements but also how observation of test participants builds lasting empathy and understanding of heretofore faceless online audiences. Reference professionals have already been cultivating this empathy and understanding for years. Though research methods are evolving rapidly, human nature hasn't much changed, and reference staff have always had a front-row seat for observing patrons' desires. For example, academic researchers (such as art historians) frequently express concern over the possibility of "missing something" in the archives—failing to locate or identify a vital document that could represent an important discovery for their discipline. Online, this concern might have implications for the way the site search engine is expected to work—with researchers favoring greater recall over finer precision, perhaps. Experience witnessing patterns of researcher behavior can make reference staff especially adept at identifying common issues and tendencies when observing usability test participants.

Both quantitative and qualitative user research are required in order to understand how a website is working for users. For examples and best practices in conducting our studies, we rarely turn to the archival literature (which contains relatively few published examples of usability studies) and instead stay abreast of best practices through the commercial web design and UX communities and the books, blogs, and podcasts they publish. From these communities we know that consistency and simplicity are the keys to a successful design. We know that search engine optimization is vital to remaining findable and relevant. And we also know that we constantly need to be in a virtuous circle of testing and iterative improvements.

To help gather information on our users, we have a long-term satisfaction survey running on our website, and we regularly monitor and analyze web traffic and search patterns using Google Analytics and Google Webmaster Tools. We rely on these tools to understand what type of content is most popular on our site, the paths that people take to find us, and to see how long they stayed. However, when we look at how much time users spend on a particular set of collections-related pages, we usually have no way of contextualizing their activity. Do people spend a longer time on finding aid pages because they are engaged with what they are reading, or could they be confused and taking a while to puzzle it all out? This is where the qualitative aspect of user-centered design and its related techniques comes into play. Usability testing is at the heart of the process.

Before we began designing our first usability test, we had to take a step back and identify our key audiences. Each year the archives' reference services staff fields over 2,500 research inquiries from all over the world. We spend many hours reading through hundreds of requests and identifying the major groups into which these inquiries fall. With this knowledge of our users in mind, we developed a group of "personas" — fictional characters used to represent the different user types we know make use of our collections.[1] Each of these types has their own expectations of how they should be able to use our site. For example, an archivist in training may want to consult a group of finding aids to study their structure, a publishing assistant may need a particular high-resolution image (ASAP!), while an art historian working on a Ph.D. thesis will be most interested in a spending time with a single finding aid related to the painter who is the subject of his or her research. Constructing our personas was an exercise of the imagination that helped shift the focus away from personal preferences.

One ongoing challenge is trying to recruit test participants consistent with the types that we identified as using our actual website. This means they fit the rough age and education ranges of our users but are not employees, interns, friends, or relatives, all of whom carry some bias. Due to budget rules, we were told we could not compensate test participants financially as professional usability test recruiters do. We therefore learned how to get creative with incentives, giving away books by our curator and copies of our print *Journal* as a means of thanking participants for their time. While we have posted flyers and approached strangers cold, we have also drawn from the ranks of the larger Smithsonian network of volunteers and art history research fellows. Sometimes we have participants make an appointment, but most often we just show up at a gathering place (e.g., a lounge frequented by graduate students) and see if any potential participants are available right at that moment.

Because we are part of the Smithsonian Institution, we were required to complete training related to human-subjects research and submit our project for review by the Institutional Review Board (IRB), a process frequently required in an academic setting. Having our research approved by the IRB was required to ensure that we would have the option to publish our findings. Additionally, we wanted to make sure that we had full knowledge and consent to record the sessions with our participants and gave priority consideration to their rights and privacy concerns.

IMPLEMENTATION

A usability test is not the same as a focus group—it aims for less talk, more action. It is hard to get honest, meaningful verbal feedback on an existing web interface. This is why user experience expert Jakob Nielsen's oft-quoted "first rule of usability" is to *ignore what users say, and watch what they do.*[2] The unreliability of self-reporting has certainly been confirmed in our own experiences at the archives. There have been many times we have watched a participant flail his or her way through a test, struggling over every task, only to announce at the conclusion "Your website is really great! I like it a lot." Are they just trying to be nice? Are their expectations too low? The truth is that users nearly always blame themselves, not the website, for any navigational difficulties they run across. It would be tempting to believe their compliments if we hadn't just watched them struggling with our own eyes.

Therefore, we don't typically do a lot of interviewing of our test participants. Instead, we sit them down in front of a computer and have them get them started working on a list of various tasks using the Archives of American Art's website. Typical tasks from past tests have included a mix of questions, both easy and challenging, such as:

- You would like to visit the Archives of American Art. Where is it located? When can you visit?
- You would like to read the transcript of Archives of American Art's interview with Helen Frankenthaler. How would you do that?
- Can you find a picture of the sculptor Una Hanbury?

The job of the test facilitator is to gently keep the participant focused on the tasks and be available to acknowledge—but not necessarily answer—any questions that the participant may have. Mostly, she tries very hard to stay neutral and inexpressive in order to avoid nudging the participant toward any particular outcomes or conclusions. Her main verbalization is to remind the participants to share their thoughts out loud as they go through the tasks by saying "What are you thinking right now?"

Our methodology is built around the classic do-it-yourself usability testing model described by Steve Krug in his books *Don't Make Me Think* and *Rocket Surgery Made Easy*[3] and by Jeffrey Rubin and Dana Chisnell's *Handbook of Usability Testing.*[4] We try to keep the testing and the reporting process lightweight and practical so that it is not a burden on us to test and retest often.

In some recent rounds of testing, we have modified Krug's approach slightly to incorporate the addition of some "interview-based tasks" as described by Jared Spool. We have found that Spool's innovation in task assignment helps increase the motivation level of our volunteer participants by building on their existing research interests and enthusiasms.[5] For example, if we are testing a graduate student, the test facilitator might ask him what his dissertation is about and have him look to see if there are any resources in the Archives of American Art that might be useful for his research.

However, we always have a scripted list of user tasks inspired by real-life reference questions. The interactions that the reference team has with our patrons are a kind of frontline "market research" about what our audiences want and need. By using reference questions to inspire our testing tasks, we keep the focus on what users are actually doing on our website (and not just what we think or assume they *should* be doing). Before composing a new test script, we sit down with a list of submitted questions from recent months and read through them, looking for typical patterns and wording. We like to borrow language directly from researchers in writing the tasks rather than using our own terminology.

The reference team at the archives has the closest and most personal form of daily contact with our researchers. They hear all of the compliments and complaints in researchers' true voices, and they know how the collections and finding aids are used and interpreted. When it came to making website improvements, bringing the technological and web design expertise into close conversation with reference expertise was a key moment. The dynamic between the two departments as we came together was not about reference asking web/IT to make changes to the website based on their needs, nor was it about web/IT needing stakeholder stamp of approval on their decisions. Rather, we made a choice to create a new usability program in tandem, with the shared goal of turning the entire organization's focus outward. The ongoing usability testing program at the archives is a joint partnership between reference and web/IT staff, with participation and support from processing archivists and curatorial staff.

By inviting every department across the archives to view usability tests—either from a remote viewing room, while the tests are in process, or, later, at an all-staff review session—and help evaluate the results, we have gradually changed the focus of our conversations from being organization-centric to being more user-centric. The questions we have always asked ourselves about our website (e.g., What categories belong in the global navigation? What features should the image viewer window have?) have started leading back to one big one: How are real researchers impacted by this? We make tweaks or prototypes and find the answers to our questions by running usability tests.

Our first round of testing, in 2007, involved no special technological tools or software. We weren't just low tech; we were no tech! To make the case for the value of usability studies and our commitment to running them, we conducted our first round of testing using nothing more than a borrowed office workstation, paper and pencils, and our powers of observation.

Because we did not have access to software to record this first round of test sessions, a group of archivist colleagues acted as observers, sitting behind the test participants and taking notes (as quietly and unobtrusively as possible) about which aspects of the website were giving the participants the most trouble. These observer notes and the discussions we had between sessions were synthesized into our first web usability report. While the in-person observer technique is less than ideal, it was still better than the alternative at that time, which would been no usability testing at all. Despite the constraints, just one round of usability testing revealed some areas of priority for improvement, such as improving the consistency and clarity of our global navigation, and problems with the relevancy ranking of results returned by our search box.

Completing our first, "no-tech" round of usability testing and producing a useful report demonstrated our commitment and the utility of the process. Funds were subsequently made available to purchase a dedicated laptop, TechSmith's Morae software, a microphone, and a webcam, all of which helped us professionalize our usability endeavors. We have found that having specialized software has been critical to the long-term success of our program. Particularly, we appreciate the ability to record and review video with a picture-in-picture view of the test participant (see figure 12.1) and features that indicate when and where on the screen the participant is clicking and using his or her mouse. Apart from the initial outlay for this equipment and software, the only ongoing expenses are staff time and the publications we give away as incentives for participation.

As we fine-tuned our infrastructure and methods through repeated rounds of tests, we also sought to broaden the audience segments we were recruiting. In our early rounds of testing, all test participants were graduate students or professors with specializations in the fields of American art and history. However, because we receive many inquiries from nonscholars, we felt it was important to have user data from other demographics as well.

The Archives of American Art's Washington, DC, research center is across the street from the Donald W. Reynolds Center for American Art and Portraiture, which features a large, covered courtyard space (with WiFi access) and is heavily trafficked during the lunch hour. Our laptop with the Morae Recorder software installed became our "mobile usability

Figure 12.1.   Screen capture, with picture-in-picture, of a participant interacting with the Archives of American Art's website during a usability test.

lab," and we were able to recruit participants from the courtyard as they drifted in and out of the cafe and museums. Working with a mobile lab presented some challenges. The noise levels of a large public space are not conducive to high-quality sound recording. Additionally, because we were outside of our office suite and not connected to a computer that had the Morae Observer software running, we did not have the advantage of having simultaneous remote observation and automated task logging. Not having that data added more work on the reporting end of this round of testing. We could not easily call up all the responses to a specific task but had to go through each video (which usually range from thirty to forty-five minutes) and note time stamps in order to make an illustrative set of clips to add to a conference presentation.[6]

While we did return to our practice of using scholars in subsequent rounds of testing—they continue to be a core constituency and one of our primary audiences—we also turned to the Smithsonian Institution's volunteer program for help in recruiting our non–subject specialist participants, specifically of retirement age. We scheduled eight individuals, relying on a telephone-based preinterview process to select the most appropriate participants. In both of these examples, it took an additional effort to recruit outside of our usual community of scholars, but because we know from our surveys that nonscholars and researchers of retirement age are significant segments of our user population, we would be remiss if we neglected them.

Our tasks lists have evolved over time, as has our methodology. We now regularly include a mix of scripted tasks and interview-based tasks, depending on the background of the participant. We plan to continue broadening our demographic target to include a wide range of researcher ages and backgrounds. In the future we also want to explore new technologies to enable more frequent testing outside of our immediate geographic region, including options for remotely hosted usability testing online, both facilitated and automated.

RESULTS

While we initially had to make the case for a usability program, after completing a few rounds of testing and circulating our reports widely, we have found a supportive culture for our efforts. In addition to written reports, at the end of every round of testing, we hold a video screening for all interested staff and interns. We provide coffee and donuts (incentives are important!) and screen the video recordings in our conference room. These events are casual gatherings where our colleagues are free to drift in and out or stay for the duration. These sessions have had a huge impact, not only in attitudes toward improving the online user experience but also in how we respond to our researchers.

As archivists we tend to use quite a bit of jargon. We sometimes forget that terminology can vary from repository to repository and that researchers might not understand our specialized terms. It can be hard to remember that the facile search we perform in a specialized catalog every day as part of our job can be challenging or confusing to a researcher. Given the complex nature of archival collections, using archives can be a challenge even with a user-friendly website. When one sees these struggles playing back via the video capture, however, it can build great empathy for the researcher. And this, in turn, helps us serve them better. This growth in empathy is especially apparent in staff and interns who do not work directly with researchers as part of their regular duties. As Louis Rosenfeld and Peter Morville put it, "When it comes to developing empathy for the user, remember that there's no substitute for being in the same room."[7]

Holding screenings for staff has allowed us to demystify the usability testing process for them as well as provided a forum for questions and discussion. While we often come away from these sessions with long to-do lists of things we would like to fix or change, sharing our research also allows us to highlight what is working well. It shines a light onto the positive outcomes of the hard work that everyone at the Archives of American Art does, from accessing and processing collections to serving them to researchers, digitally or otherwise.

For example, we focused a recent round of tests specifically on the use of finding aids. When we screened the videos, some of the archivists in the room looked rapt: They had never actually seen a researcher making use of their primary product on the web before. It was a novel pleasure for them to hear remarks about how the page was "well organized," and they took notice when a nonscholar was able to intuit what *series* signified. The mood changed, however, when one of the users was assigned the task of finding a set of images from the collection. The recording showed that she failed to locate the link to the digital materials. Some viewers responded audibly, "But the link is right there!" One reference professional who was in the room shook her head but admitted that she was not surprised. She said that she had been on the telephone with seasoned researchers before and had to walk them through, click by click, to access a certain digitized collection. Positively, though, the reference department reports a drop in self-serve requests and questions about website navigation on the whole since the usability program has been in place.

Finally, it was vitally important that the supervisory staff of both the reference and web/IT departments demonstrated their commitment to the program by adding usability testing to our "official duties." This has established it as an ongoing initiative. We continue to collaborate and attribute our success to partnering across departmental lines to harness our expertise in technology *and* in people.

LESSONS LEARNED

After six years of collaborating on the archives' usability program, we have learned firsthand about the rewards and the pitfalls. One important lesson is that writing effective tasks for the usability test script takes time and practice. We consciously avoid jargon and leading words; for example, we don't use key navigation menu categories like *collections* as a word in the task itself. We include a mix of easy and hard tasks so that participants do not become fatigued or discouraged. Often, instead of asking the participant a direct question like, "Can you find the Florence Arquin papers?" we might ask them to answer some other question that relies on content that may appear within Arquin's finding aid or collection record. We have also found it useful to try out the tasks and software internally on staff and interns before a new round of testing to ensure that everything operates correctly and to get a sense of how long it will take for a participant to complete all the tasks. Just remember that these internal users' results should not be considered valid because anyone who works for your organization (even if it is just for the summer) knows *way* too much about your website to be considered a "normal" user.

We have also learned how to overcome our normal habits of being helpful and inquiring in order to act as effective test facilitators. A reference specialist spends considerable energy each day helping people find what they are looking for, so it can be very tough for that same person to suddenly turn around and sit, quiet and inexpressive, next to a user who is struggling to understand the archives' online collections. At the beginning of each test, the facilitator tells our participants, "If you have a question, please voice it out loud, though I may not be able to answer." Not answering—not even reacting with facial expressions that show approval or disapproval—can be a struggle, but a neutral attitude is essential for the facilitator to be effective.

In addition, we have learned a great deal about the effectiveness and importance of usability software. The ability to record and share video makes the process much more effective and doesn't have to be a major financial investment. After a thirty-day free trial, we chose to purchase Morae because it is robust, with effective picture-in-picture capture, task annotation, and click-highlighting animation. Because it was designed specifically for usability testing, it does everything that we need it to do.

Some people also use Camtasia Studio ($300), also from TechSmith, as a cheaper alternative to Morae. It doesn't offer all of the same features, but it will capture screen activity and sound effectively. If you have a Mac, Silverback is also an extremely effective and inexpensive software option at $69.

When compared to what it would cost to pay a usability consultant to come and do a round of testing for you, we would argue that buying our own software and conducting the tests ourselves was actually a major bargain. In the long run, usability testing can save money because you are able to be strategic about which improvements to your website offer the biggest gains to your researchers. Without it, you might waste resources trying to "fix" pieces of your website that aren't actually broken while ignoring small but vital improvements that might have a major impact on your researchers. Additionally, the DIY usability testing method has a team-building benefit. We share a sense of pride in having created a successful cross-departmental collaboration and feel good about our focus on making researchers' work a little bit easier. The videos show how clearly reference work connects with that of IT professionals and archivists and help remind everyone that we all serve the needs of real people with real questions. The conversations we have at these screenings are a rare opportunity to candidly discuss the overlap and the divide between the areas of responsibility in our jobs.

We have also learned to keep our reporting and documentation light-weight, actionable, and focused on prioritizing the low-hanging fruit. Elaborate reporting can quickly turn into a burden. We feel it is better to produce a one- to two-page list of improvements we actually have a chance of implementing than to write a ten-page report that is just going to sit in a drawer. In this way we reserve our time and energy for doing additional tests and for implementing the suggested improvements to the website.

More than anything, our greatest lesson learned was the importance of just jumping right in and doing it! Rather than spending a lot of time discussing how we wanted to start usability testing, we just started usability testing. Recruiting strangers was a bit intimidating at first, and we made mistakes along the way, of course, but we were able to learn by trial and error. We have gotten better at usability testing by doing usability testing—over and over, again and again.

CONCLUSION

The ultimate goal of our program is to use realistic situations drawn from reference interactions to find out what aspects of the Archives of American Art's website are working for our researchers. It is a pragmatic, low-overhead, incremental approach to improving our digital collections interface, but the cumulative knowledge of our audiences we have gained through the years heavily informs our digital projects. The program represents not only a close collaboration between reference and web/IT staff but also incorporates the help and input of archivists throughout the organization. In this way, helping online researchers is not seen as the responsibility of any single department; it is everyone's job. The more empathy and understanding we can develop for our online users, the better positioned we are to prioritize refining our online interfaces to be centered on their needs.

As the web has become the primary access point to our collections for researchers around the world, our websites serve as a digital extension of reference. Finding a reliable archival interface that is pleasant to interact with is analogous to walking into the reading room and meeting an expert reference archivist with a welcoming smile. The websites and the people have to work in tandem in order to create a seamless and positive experience for researchers. Archival collections are inherently complex, but the way users interact with them doesn't have to be. Creating digital access points that are easy to use helps researchers, but it also can relieve the burden on reference staff to answer simple questions and let them reserve their time and expertise for more important matters.

Sara Snyder is the webmaster and Elizabeth Botten is an archives specialist, Reference Services, at the Archives of American Art, Smithsonian Institution.

NOTES

1. For a brief description of how to create and use personas as part of a user-centered design process, see "Personas," *Usability.gov*, accessed July 21, 2013, www.usability.gov/how-to-and-tools/methods/personas.html.

2. Jakob Nielsen, "First Rule of Usability? Don't Listen to Users," *Nielsen Norman Group*, August 5, 2001, accessed July 20, 2013, www.nngroup.com/articles/first-rule-of-usability-dont-listen-to-users.

3. Steve Krug, *Don't Make Me Think! A Common Sense Approach to Web Usability* (Berkeley, CA: New Riders Pub, 2006); Steve Krug, *Rocket Surgery Made Easy: The Do-It-Yourself Guide to Finding and Fixing Usability Problems* (Berkeley, CA: New Riders, 2010).

4. Jeffrey Rubin and Dana Chisnell, *Handbook of Usability Testing: How to Plan, Design, and Conduct Effective Tests* (Hoboken, NJ: John Wiley and Sons, 2008).

5. Jared M. Spool, "Interview-Based Tasks: Learning from Leonardo DiCaprio," *User Interface Engineering*, March 7, 2006, accessed May 1, 2013, www.uie.com/articles/interview_based_tasks; Jared Spool, "Usability Tools Podcast: Interview-Based Tasks for Usability Testing," *User Interface Engineering*, October 1, 2007, accessed May 1, 2013, www.uie.com/brainsparks/2007/10/01/usability-tools-podcast-interview-based-tasks-for-usability-testing.

6. We spoke about these early tests and how they informed our web redesign project at the Society of American Archivists 2010 annual meeting (Washington, DC) as part of the panel "That Was Easy: Making Digital Archives a Pleasure to Use."

7. Louis Rosenfeld and Peter Morville, *Information Architecture for the World Wide Web Designing Large-Scale Websites* (Sebastopol, CA: O'Reilly Media, 2008), 361.

Index

About the Editor

Kate Theimer is the author of the popular blog *ArchivesNext* and a frequent writer, speaker, and commentator on issues related to the future of archives. She is the author of *Web 2.0 Tools and Strategies for Archives and Local History Collections* and the editor of *A Different Kind of Web: New Connections between Archives and Our Users*, as well having contributed chapters to *Many Happy Returns: Advocacy for Archives and Archivists*, *The Future of Archives and Recordkeeping*, and the forthcoming *Encyclopedia of Archival Concepts, Principles, and Practices*. She has published articles in *The American Archivist* and the *Journal of Digital Humanities*.

Kate served on the Council of the Society of American Archivists from 2010 to 2013. Before starting her career as an independent writer and editor, she worked in the policy division of the National Archives and Records Administration in College Park, Maryland. She holds an MSI with a specialization in archives and records management from the University of Michigan and an MA in art history from the University of Maryland.